LEADING THROUGH THE PANDEMIC

UNCONVENTIONAL WISDOM FROM HEARTFELT LEADERS

SOUL EXCELLENCE

CONTENTS

Introduction   vii

1. Amy Pittman   I
Your Position Is Being Eliminated...Again

2. Andrea McDowell   I I
Lead Yourself First

3. Ashish Bisaria   23
Leading from a Different Point of View

4. Brendan Daly   33
The Purpose of Purpose

5. Brittany Perkins Castillo   45
Never Not Working: How to Lead in an Environment of Constant Crisis

6. Chandra Gundlapalli   55
Lead with Humility (Not a Hierarchy) With an Empowered Champion of Champions Operating Model

7. Chantée L. Christian   67
My Best SHIFT

8. Deepak Jose   77
Episode 2020: Importance of Self Reflection to Reaffirm, Realize, and Reinvent

9. Hannah Stenning   89
Leading Through the Pandemic While Reporting On It

10. James Gilbert   99
We Are All Human

11. James Jackson, III   109
A Leadership Ability Unveiled

12. Jennifer Anglin   119
Manufactured Results

13. Kasia Hein-Peters   129
Leading with Science (and Sometimes with Science-Fiction)

14. Marc Snyderman   139
Finding My Why in Turbulent Times

11. Marissa Snow   149
The Collapse

12. Michelle E. Clark   155
2020 Perfect Vision: Lessons from a Sandwich

13. Paul Smith   165
A Rollercoaster of Emotions

14. Ram Iyer   177
My Leadership Lessons from the Pandemic and Baking Bread

15. Rick Ricardo   187
Purpose and Progress Through this Pandemic

16. Sasha Stair   197
2020, A Solar Eclipse

17. Suzanne O'Brien   207
Great Expectations; New Reality

18. Tina Gravel   215
From 5-Star Hotels to 5-Hours on Zoom

19. Vivian Cintron   223
RESILIENCE… The Ability to Adapt and Bounce FORWARD

24. Wyatt Knight   233
    1% Better Everyday

25. About the Publisher   241

INTRODUCTION

I'm Kayleigh Marie O'Keefe, CEO and Founder of Soul Excellence Publishing and the woman who has brought together the leaders in this book.

This book almost didn't happen. Why? I succumbed to the fear of the unknown. Instead of blazing my own trail, I sought comfort, safety, and the familiar.

In January, I committed to launching Soul Excellence Ventures. The term had come into my mind just a couple of months before, and it so intrigued me that I knew it was time to explore. I told my VP at the flourishing tech start-up that I worked at that I would be leaving. He couldn't quite understand my decision, though encouraged me to follow my dream. I registered the LLC, designed the logo, and moved across the country, from California to my home state of Florida, on February 29th, leap day.

As we took off and the plane did one stunning last loop over San Francisco — the fog just beginning to recede and reveal the international orange of the Golden Gate Bridge — I felt exhilarated and full of possibility.

I was going to uncover my voice after so many years of adopting a corporate one. The corporate Kayleigh voice, in retrospect, came across as strong and competent but lacked emotional depth or conviction. Beneath the directives and the decisions came neediness and a desire to be fully expressed and seen that diluted my impact.

In those first couple of weeks, I blogged. I wrote newsletters to my 'Soul Excellence Leaders.' I created a makeshift studio in my closet to record podcast episodes about my life and journey. I began to feel my heart and soul expand. I began to touch and feel the edges of the box I had put myself in but hadn't realized. And I began to peek out and express. I felt free as a bird. No corporate schedule. No one to impress. And not a care for COVID-19, which I thought I had escaped when I left the West Coast.

Then the signs went up at the beach: "Beach Closed until April 12th." Days before April 12th, the bottom half of the signs had been erased, leaving "Beach Closed."

The doubt started to settle in.

I am a strong and high-achieving person by nature so it's hard to perceive when I'm afraid. Fear doesn't take the form of dread or tears. Instead, it plays out as confusion, frustration, and justification.

I allowed myself to succumb to the anxiety of the world that penetrated the air. And my initial enthusiasm for Soul Excellence gave way to practical concerns.

Maybe this isn't the best year to launch a business, I reasoned.

Maybe it would be safer to earn a salary, vest equity, and receive high-quality health insurance, just for this year, I told myself.

And so I applied for and got a job within a week to build out a local team for a Seattle-based tech insurance company expanding into Medicare.

I didn't want to admit that I was afraid, so I justified the decision. Have you done that too this year? I'm new to Florida. I'll make new connections and meet future clients. The smart thing to do is to get a salary and benefits while I launch my side hustle!

Just two weeks into the role, I realized that I had made a terrible mistake.

I was on the phone all day trying to recruit and onboard insurance agents to our platform, hardly my forte or what the role had promised. I was grateful that I had purchased a desk and a comfy work chair as home office supplies were gobbled up and went on backorder for months. A poster of my newly crafted Values and Principles document lorded over me at my desk, daily prodding me to consider — am I pursuing and embodying what matters most to me right now — trust, courage, fun, action, and joy?

My eyes moved back and forth on the screen from Zoom to Slack and Slack to Zoom. I conducted nearly forty interviews to hire for our rapidly growing team. The vision for a homegrown team in the company's new office space gave way overnight to a remote workforce.

Key decisions were made on Slack at 10 PM — and required instant communication out to the team the next morning. I had been on the senior leadership team for Snapdocs, informing our key decisions and crafting how best to communicate them to the company, and now I felt the squeeze of being a new hire in middle management.

Still, I saw the places where I lit up — preparing for our team meetings, setting the context for the week's priorities, problem-solving on the fly, and reenergizing after a hard day.

And I built an instant, deep friendship with my fellow team leader. I'd walk the block at the end of the day, and she would pace in her backyard as we vented, strategized, and wondered how on earth we could hit our audacious hiring and commercial goals.

I was then three days into a physical detox, when I felt like I was given a new pair of contacts and could make out the leaves on the trees again. I received immediate clarity for what I had to do.

And so I told my boss that I was leaving, and I agreed to stay on for three weeks to staff and lead the team to prepare them for our next phase of growth.

It is natural to seek safety in times of uncertainty.

But if you're reading this book — you are a leader. You are not like everyone else. You are not a sheep. You are the shepherd of your family, community, colleagues, and teams.

Once I fully owned who I was — and expressed what I desired — the world began to respond.

I wrote a chapter in a best-selling book, and the concept of Soul Excellence exited my mind and entered the universe of ideas.

I created my Soul Excellence Leadership framework, a way to guide leaders out of their old patterns and into a more expressed, aligned, and fulfilled version of themselves to lead fearlessly through uncertainty.

And, I launched the publishing arm of the company that has published this insightful book of diverse perspectives in leadership.

Here is my hope for you, dear reader: Awaken to your desire. Stay the course. Trust yourself.

This year, we were told to trust the experts, the scientists, the politicians.

And in many cases, they failed us. They acted hypocritically, deciding which rules applied to them. Which means it is up to you and me — to the Soul Excellence Leaders — to step up. To discern. To think critically. To respond. To speak. To inspire. As you read these stories of personal transformation, awakening, and growth, I invite you to consider -

How can you create more space to tap into your inner wisdom?

This book will reveal the skills required of 21st-century leadership — soul integration, courageous innovation, divine inspiration, and intentional initiation — these are the pillars of your personal expression of Soul Excellence Leadership.

Shine brightly,
Kayleigh Marie O'Keefe

AMY PITTMAN

YOUR POSITION IS BEING ELIMINATED...AGAIN

"To be human is to be vulnerable.
To be a leader is to be vulnerable every day, every moment.
That's leadership."
– Brené Brown

Prior to the COVID-19 pandemic reaching the U.S. in March of 2020, I lived through five of the Top Ten most stressful life changes a person can experience – all within a two-year span.

I know first-hand that it can be difficult to live out your values in the face of fear and disappointment because it's been the crucible for connecting me to my courage and integrity.

From the late fall of 2017 through the summer of 2019, I survived a job layoff after 9 years of dedicated service to a now dismantled franchise, followed by eighteen turbulent months of engaging my networks seeking new work opportunities. I picked up a few interesting consulting projects along the way, but failed to secure sustainable full-time work despite a stellar history of work performance and strong connections. Having drained my life savings in the process, I made the difficult decision to sell my home in San Diego, California. Before the closing date arrived, I suffered the death of my beloved 11-year-old Labrador, Baxter. Then, I shattered part of my left hand in an unfortunate barbell accident at the gym.

Grief-stricken over the loss of a meaningful life I had spent nearly a decade purposefully cultivating, I was in need of love, healing and rest. Feeling defeated and quite literally broken, my friends rallied around me to pack up what was left of my life and I drove myself over 2,000 miles across the country to reunite with family in the suburbs of Detroit.

Back home in Michigan, I was surrounded by the support and comfort I so desperately needed and I forged ahead. Soon, I was recruited by a mentor of mine from early in my career to return to work for a values-driven, family-owned food service distribution company based in Grand Rapids. I had worked for this company for almost nine years prior to moving west in 2008, and now, the company's need to grow their Learning & Development team due to ongoing expansion into new markets across the U.S. aligned with the skills in management, leadership and employee training I had cultivated throughout my career. It was a perfect fit and the timing was right for me to return to the company as a Divisional Sales Trainer.

The upside to that unexpectedly long, grueling period of job searching was a deepening clarity of my priorities, interests, and talents, which in turn, helped expand and empower my choices. I learned that I am an explorer at heart and thrive on travel and meeting new people, and excel in environments with rapid growth. So, despite having the option to be based in my hometown division near Detroit, I made the courageous choice to take a chance on growth in the unfamiliar territory of Charlotte, North Carolina.

A profoundly deep sense of relief washed over me, as *this* was the change in circumstances I had been praying for. So, in July of 2019 my childhood best friend drove with me from Detroit to Charlotte for my official relocation and a fresh start. I felt as though I had turned a corner in the stressful, yet hopeful process of re-establishing stability in my life after a prolonged period of transition.

In my career as a Sales & Leadership Development Trainer, I rely heavily on collaborative relationships with others, and so relationship-building was my first priority upon arriving on the job. To build trust and rapport quickly, I rely on my genuine care for others and my curiosity around their experiences and perspectives to ask questions, probe for clarity, and listen purposefully. I prefer face-to-face interactions, opting to sit across from sales leaders in their offices and ride alongside sales reps in their territories.

There were at least sixty individuals for me to get to know in this way in the Carolinas division, along with extensively training each group of new hires that joined the company. As you can imagine, my calendar quickly filled with meetings and events, starting with sales leadership.

During my first week on the job, I witnessed behavior from certain leaders at an offsite strategic planning meeting that required a series of candid, difficult, and brave conversations. The culture was askew and I was worried I had made a huge mistake choosing a relocation with this company. I was committed to finding a resolution; again, I forged ahead. Over the next six months, further conversations with sales reps and support staff exposed the root cause of the issues that were contributing to low morale, sub-optimal performance, and high turnover rates.

Ultimately, an investigation was conducted and two sales leaders were dismissed from the company and replaced with a new leader in January of 2020. It was a tumultuous start, but I was on track to having the support necessary to be effective in my role and contribute to a healthier culture.

Eight months into establishing myself in the Carolinas, and with new leadership in place, professionally I had moved beyond the initial learning curve into confident and consistent effectiveness. I planned and executed high impact training events and was gaining momentum in my relationships and collaborations across the company. I explored many new cities within the division and was even invited to lead a workshop at a company-wide leadership symposium. I was operating in my areas of strength and having fun doing it! After returning from a week-long certification training back at headquarters in Grand Rapids, buoyed by the supportive culture I had fondly remembered at the home office, I remember posting on social media that this is what it feels like to *belong*.

On a personal level, as a long-time advocate of healthy and active living, I had developed a fitness routine around my work travels and was walking to local attractions regularly. I gained familiarity with where my favorite stores were located in Charlotte and was beginning to establish a social life. My self-care routines were in place and I was thriving once again.

Then an unpredictable, highly contagious, and deadly virus would unravel this newfound sense of stability and security.

By mid-March, the Coronavirus and the panic had spread to North Carolina when the governor ordered schools to be closed and gatherings to be limited in size. For the safety of staff, division leadership decided to move all meetings to a virtual setting until further notice. In my role this required immediate flexibility, heavy doses of faith in my facilitation skills and a willingness to be a learner in order to adapt dozens of scheduled learning events from live presentations to virtual ones overnight.

The energy required to master video conferencing tools, introduce new e-learning technologies, redesign workshop activities, and recalibrate schedules was daunting. It demanded intense focus and heavy communication to make these adjustments swiftly, while also dealing with growing fears of my own family's safety. Detroit happened to be one of the nation's early "hot spots" where the virus was spreading more rapidly and I had several family members there with compromising health conditions who would be highly susceptible to death if exposed to the virus. Yet, I forged ahead.

By the time the Stay-at-Home executive order was announced two weeks later, I had been in front of my computer 12-14 hours a day, 6 days a week responding to constant emails and calendar requests, delivering virtual new hire training workshops and preparing for upcoming sessions. Effective March 30th, the governor's order directed people to stay at home except to visit essential businesses, to exercise outdoors or to help a family member for the next 30 days – we were under strict quarantine.

This meant all dining rooms outside the home must close, which launched our customers and employees into full on crisis mode. Because our company serviced mostly independent restaurants, local chains, hospitals, schools and nursing homes, these mandated closures meant that our company lost more than half of its revenue overnight. Many of our customers wouldn't be able to recover from even temporary closures and would inevitably shut down permanently.

This brought on the first round of furloughs for our company which would impact our current new hire trainees. This was upsetting news, as I had just invested 12 weeks into onboarding these individuals and building relationships with them. Our competitors were laying off employees by the hundreds, and the industry looked grim, so I braced for news of more furloughs while I forged ahead.

Stress levels were mounting and the mass shut down had also compromised my preferred stress management strategies such as CrossFit-style workouts at the gym, socializing with friends, and exploring the city. Sleep was restless at best, resulting in an increase in coffee consumption and anxiety during the day. As I was trained to do my entire life, I was over-functioning. I was so caught up in being of service to others, that I hardly had time to slow down and pay attention to my own needs. The demand for training to keep people "busy" became overwhelming.

To be a curator, creator, and deliverer of content for an entire division under these circumstances was impossible for one person. It required collaboration. I met with managers to assess team needs and compiled lists of internal and external resources for personal and professional development. I worked with Directors of Marketing and Sales to coordinate a division-wide training calendar, advocating for turning our cameras on during video conferences to have a stronger sense of connection. I began delivering 90-minute development workshops up to three times a day on topics such as listening and having crucial conversations. I contributed to a companywide workshop on stress management strategies and how to recognize a stress response in yourself and others.

I identified ten of our top sales reps to engage as mentors, and collaborated with them to design and deliver a 5-week Peer Led Learning webinar series, the quality of which I was incredibly proud. It was a dizzying pace, yet gratifying to solve problems with others and work as a team to create something useful during a time of crisis.

On April 10th, one hour before the live launch of our first webinar session, I received the dreaded news that I was included in the next round of furloughs.

Intellectually, I understood the decision and maintained hope that this was a temporary situation, but the tears and tension tumbled out after the call with my Manager ended. As if on cue, I heard the rumble of demolition equipment outside my window. To my surprise, the foundation was being cleared for the construction of a nine-story office building directly across the street from my apartment. I thought, "great, everything is falling apart."

I felt the hangover of an intensely imbalanced focus on work for the past six weeks, and was grateful for the break to focus on myself. I went from hyper-scheduled to zero structure overnight. Luckily, I had extensive training in wellness practices, so I channeled all of this disciplined energy into prioritizing my own self-care, and once again I forged ahead.

I kept myself surprisingly busy. The stress had severely disrupted my digestive system, so each week I prepared soothing, nutritious meals. I cued up online fitness classes and made a point to get outside for a daily walk on city greenways. I lit candles, took baths, and listened to wellness podcasts. I journaled and meditated. I kept in touch with my loved ones by phone regularly and even organized a puzzle exchange with friends to satisfy my task-focused mind.

Life went on like this for thirteen more weeks. When the Stay-at-Home order was extended, twice, I became restless and agitated. As an extremely extroverted, action oriented, social creature, this was agonizing. I lived alone in a large apartment complex in the heart of a major city, but there were entire weekends where I didn't see or speak to another human being. I missed my family. I missed human contact. With the exception of going to the grocery store once a week, I needed a reason to get out of my apartment and away from the constant, nerve wracking construction noise. I felt like a caged animal.

Then, on June 26th, after nearly four months of lockdown I was officially laid-off. Now, this was no surprise and I handled the separation with my employer with grace, understanding, and a positive outlook. I had prepared myself for this possibility all along, yet the intensity of the emotional reaction I felt inside grabbed my attention – I felt shattered.

Those candlelit baths were now punctuated with weeping. I lost motivation for indoor exercise and simple pleasures. A sinking feeling washed over me as I relived the pain of my first layoff all over again. I was overcome with strong emotions such as sadness, anger, indignation and despair. I was embarrassed and ashamed of myself for having this reaction. "It was just a job!", I scolded myself, "you've been through this before, and you're not the only one suffering right now, suck it up."

Then it dawned on me: these feelings were about more than this moment, or even the previous layoff. In the stillness of quarantine, years of buried angst made its way to my conscious awareness, ready to be released. I wasn't the caged animal after all; it was unprocessed grief clawing its way out.

This grief went way back. When I was about 11 years old, my mom left us. After a blowout fight with my dad one day, she was gone. In her absence, I stepped up to help raise my 4-year-old sister while my older brother self-isolated and my father's health deteriorated due to alcoholism. We had very little interaction with Mom over the next two years until she returned home just before my father's death and my 14th birthday. This is the origin of my abandonment grief and the awakening of the leader in me.

Surprisingly, my father's death carried a simpler grief, because people rallied in support when he passed. Death is a universal loss we all understand. But abandonment by my mother? This kind of grief is complicated by a subtle and dangerous stigma – a questioning of what I must have done to deserve it. The abandonment wound cuts much deeper, causing injury to your self-worth. It's a primal kind of trauma that lingers, saying, "You're never enough." It is re-triggered over various break-ups, and in this case, separation from two employer families. I dragged this crippled self-confidence with me as I began resentfully applying to jobs again. I was clumsily over-selling myself and growing desperate as my inbox filled with rejection emails.

I allowed myself to rage in my journal. I had spent a lifetime playing by the rules to avoid the pain of such losses again and was convinced this *shouldn't* be happening. Hadn't I already paid my dues on loss in this lifetime? Why was I laid off, again, if I was as valuable as they said anyway? I wondered if maybe I was being punished for challenging leadership and advocating for a different culture. Instead of avoiding the pain, it helped me to confide in my morning pages. I could acknowledge my frustration, anger and disappointment, and release it. On paper, petty thoughts melted away to reveal wiser and gentler ones.

I hadn't afforded myself this luxury in the past. Instead, I developed a constant need to "forge ahead", which lifted me high above layers of hurt feelings. Years of achievement and a headstrong attitude had me soaring so high above the pain of childhood abandonment, that I lost connection to my ground truth. The world rewarded me for my resilience as it became rocket fuel for collecting successes for decades. Now, I was exhausted and burned out; the wins were drying up. The world said I was brave because I forged ahead, but who am I when I can no longer do so? Am I still brave?

This new awareness was not about blaming anyone else for my feelings. I became free to correctly identify the source of those hurt feelings, and claim them now as accurate guide posts to my healing. This awareness unshackled me from the shame and self-criticism I harbored as a result of having a reaction to something that is primal – the need for human connection. To be affected, especially when that primary connection is severed in formative years, is universal. It was utter reprieve to know I wasn't broken; I was merely human. And a brave one.

This realization transformed my routine of self-care into daily acts of self-love, as I began to nurture the child within that was left behind. I allowed myself to color, to create art without a purpose, to chase waterfalls all over North Carolina and play in the woods. I accepted that I had been looking for stability outside of myself, from jobs, achievements, circumstances, and now I am finding it within. I have more empathy and compassion toward others struggling with their own grief, and am able to relate from a place of authenticity.

Connecting in a loving way with my own pain instead of with judgment allowed me to ease into the uncertainty of this ongoing pandemic and remember that, even in these quieter moments, I am a courageous explorer. I traverse not only the world's landscape, but perhaps most importantly of all, my own inner landscape. The person I'm getting to know better is myself, and with that, I am experiencing exponential growth.

The process of regaining my confidence as a result of these experiences, and letting go of the life I had expected to have prior to the pandemic, is an ongoing one. So, this story doesn't have a tidy ending, other than a simple truth -- Loss is inevitable; letting go is optional.

We've all lost something to this pandemic – a loved one, a livelihood, a lifestyle, a dream, a sense of freedom or security. It's a reminder that to be human is to be vulnerable.

ABOUT THE AUTHOR

As a coach, facilitator, leadership development professional, and fellow human-being, Amy knows that true transformation starts with a decision and a dose of courage.

In Amy's chapter, she shares how the compounding effects of loss in her own life have become the compost and fertile soil for healing and personal growth, and how the pandemic in particular, transformed her practice of self-care into a deeper form of self-love.

Her passion for facilitating the journey of transformation began in 2008 as a certified weight control counselor. She spent her time coaching individuals in behavioral lifestyle changes to achieve and sustain healthy weight loss with a weight management franchise. Her most memorable client success story is a woman who lost 140 pounds in ten months!

Today, Amy blends 20 years of experience across various industries in customer service, sales, frontline operations, business management and leadership development with her talent for public speaking by leading global workshops that ignite inspired connection and spark positive change.

In her free time, Amy is an explorer in every sense of the word. She loves reading, any form of physical fitness, nature and traveling. She has driven across the U.S. four times, taking hikes in dozens of National Parks along the way.

Website: *www.WhatWouldAGrownUpDo.com*
LinkedIn: *www.linkedin.com/in/amymariepittman*

2

ANDREA MCDOWELL

LEAD YOURSELF FIRST

NEW YEARS EVE 2019

The year 2019 was huge for me, personally and professionally. On New Years Eve I decided to honour the year that was (2019) and the year that would be (2020) by saying 'no' to plans with others and 'yes' to reflection with myself.

I curled up with a cup of tea and my partner in crime: my journal.

I reflected on 2019—what I had gained, what I had learnt, what I had lost and what I was still figuring out.

I then wrote about my plans and dreams for 2020—the year of new opportunities, of taking my career to the next level, of establishing myself in my career and identity.

I have always loved planning, but my life has consistently reminded me that plans rarely materialize. Ironic, isn't it? Why? Because life happens. Years like 2020 take place and global pandemics (however far fetched they may have seemed a few years ago) are not just something that you learn about in history. They (as we learnt this year) are a reality today.

2020 started like any other year: with a month by month plan, a clear set of goals and an exciting adventure to Peru thrown in the middle. I was in a job I loved—busier than ever—living in a beautiful location. I had big plans for 2020 to be the year that I showed the world who I really was.

Studying Business Psychology unlocked the leadership geek in me, with quotes stuck on any surface that I can find, and a readiness to engage in a conversation with practically anyone about their workplace culture, dynamics and leadership.

One of my key mentors in leadership is my dad, David McDowell, who—for as long as I can remember—has shared the importance of being authentically human in the workplace. This year, I knew I needed to share my passion with the world, but I didn't know how. A podcast? A business? A book? A promotion? I entered 2020 uncertain what this new adventure would look like, but certain that it was going to happen.

LEADERSHIP FOUNDATIONS

Before we proceed, there are three key foundational elements to any leader (in my opinion). These are the three governing rules for my leadership journey.

1. **Be human:** You're kidding yourself if you think otherwise.
2. **Be you:** Your way of thinking is your point of difference so share it with the world.
3. **Be coachable:** You can always be better. Always.

FROM BUZZ WORD TO BUSINESS ACUMEN

I didn't expect that 2020 would be the year that would require leaders around the world to really step up. In all my research, I had not found any guidance on how to lead through a pandemic. Never. Ever.

This was the year that true leaders were put to the test, where buzz words such as 'agility' and concepts such as 'flexible work' went from 'nice to have' to 'need to have.' It was a year that leaders had to step up and lead their followers through a crisis rather than a strategy or project.

It was a year when leaders had to consider the comprehensive nature of what it meant to be human, in contrast to only considering what it meant to be an employee. It was a year where work-life balance transformed into work-life cohesion.

2020 was a year of giving, a year of servant leadership, and a year of responding to a global crisis. I never took that class. They don't teach you how to do that in business school.

THE ADVICE HAS BEEN IN THE WRONG ORDER FOR LEADERS

While much of the world and literature focused on what leaders had to do to serve their organisations and people, I watched in amazement as to how little guidance was provided on how leaders should lead themselves.

Leaders had to step up for others, but in doing so, often stepped away from who they were and how they were coping. As the world changed around us, leaders had to translate these changes to their teams whilst processing the events themselves. Leaders had to shift their focus hourly: people, culture, strategy, headcount, budget, business planning, health, safety, policies, the list goes on. And I wondered, did leaders have a moment to turn inward and explore how they were feeling amidst the non-stop demands on their time?

Did leaders have time to adjust to working from home?

Did anyone ask leaders how they were doing?

Did leaders have the chance to grieve team members they had to let go?

Don't get me wrong, I'm all for servant leadership. I believe the best leaders strive to serve their people, but I also believe that they are self-aware. So how, after a year like no other, can we ensure that leaders are not only finding time to understand their people, industry and organisation, but most importantly, to understand themselves?

The advice around serving others has been amazing, but if you serve others from an uncertain and unstable foundation within, you are not serving to the best of your ability.

The best leaders I know are deeply self-aware, compelled by their values, and aware of the strengths and weaknesses. They are fully aware of how to cope when times get tough (because as we've seen, times do get tough). To get to a place of knowing and deeply understanding yourself in these many facets requires time, introspection, and vulnerability.

AGENDA: *YOU* MEET *YOU*

Welcome to the first meeting with yourself. Let us cover off the key questions on the agenda.

Please answer the following agenda items:

- What are your values? ... Why? (What are the values that drive, guide, and keep you aligned?)
- What really annoys you? ... Why? (Little things, big things, characteristics, ability?)
- When are you happiest? ... Why? (When are you in flow, at peace, and most present?)
- What motivates you? ... Why? (Places, people, power?)
- How do you cope with stress and anxiety? (What practice and habits are in place?)
- Is your ego in check? (Who do you think you are better than, worthy of, and what do you think you are worthy of? Why?)

I ask these questions — not to throw you into an identity crisis — but to highlight that you may (or may not) have a few blind spots.

The reality is if you can't answer the above questions for yourself individually, how can you expect to guide your team to answering and solving them? This does not mean having it all sorted but that there needs to be an open and ongoing dialogue between *you* and *you* around understanding how to answer the above questions. In doing so, you build a strong foundation for yourself, your relationships, and your ability to lead.

WHERE IS THE ANSWER SHEET?

Unlike many other areas in organisations where you can outsource, delegate or dig up answers and clues, that is not something I can offer you for the above questions. The answer sheet lies with you and ironically, it is blank, ready for you to figure out the answers yourself. It is only with time, intention and conscious thought that answers will fill this page.

THERE WILL BE TWO LEADERS THAT COME OUT OF 2020

1. Leader one: A leader who considers 2020 a project that is now 'complete.'
2. Leader two: A leader who considers 2020 a year of learning. They will allow it (key) to shape them into new, better, and more enlightened leaders.

The difference between leader one and leader two will be whether they take the time to reflect on the year: the moments that they nailed and the moments when they tripped and fell. They will then ask a key question 'why' and they will look within for that answer.

There are several ways to do this, but the mechanism that I have found most powerful, accessible, and economical is to journal.

MY COACH, MY PARTNER IN CRIME, MY MENTOR... MY JOURNAL

I have always been an avid journaler. I have been a (self-proclaimed) overthinker for as long as I can remember. My thoughts race like there is a prize on the line. On top of this, I have always been incredibly sensitive— and my parents will confirm this. I used to see this as a negative characteristic but it is now what I love most about myself. I feel things so deeply, and I connect with others and their stories to the point where I feel like they are my own and this has allowed me to experience a rich and insightful life. However, this comes with its highs and lows, but it also provides me with heightened empathy, creativity, and an ability to read a room, to notice vibes and to decipher a situation.

I have gone through a long journey of personal development to improve my mental health, to improve as an individual and to cope with my overactive mind. My number one tool through this journey of self-discovery and self-betterment has been a series of cheap journals and pens (that I likely 'accidentally' took from a waiting room).

In the year 2020, I have completed an average of one journal per month. I have written, drawn, scribbled, listed, mind mapped, and expressed all that this year has been onto blank pages that helped me translate experience into learning. Journaling has been a consistent outlet for me: a place where I enter a zone of curiosity, openness to learning, and willingness to question myself and the world around me. A pen and empty pages have taught me more about myself than any leadership course, therapist, or personality test ever has.

We are often told that we learn from experiences. My response to that is "yes...but..."

Experiences *without* reflection are simply moments in time.
Experiences *with* reflection are game-changers.

Therefore, what you are likely thinking now is, 'Okay, that sounds great.' Reflection is important. However, what does it require? Time. What is the one thing that everyone in this world is short of? Time.

TIME IS NOT THE PROBLEM... PRIORITIES ARE.

If I had a dollar for every time I heard, "But Andrea... I have no time," I would be writing this out of my beachside bungalow rather than a suburban cafe. I will say what I say to everyone: "There is so much inequality in this world... but time does not fall into that sphere." We literally have the same amount of time every day as every other person. How we spend it is driven by our priorities and our perceptions of what we consider important.

I journal for five to ten minutes each morning and usually twenty to thirty minutes over the weekend. I spend more time on social media, browsing LinkedIn, and checking my emails.

The reality is that if the way you spend your time corresponds to what you consider important. I have made a decision that I want to live a life where I understand who I am, how I navigate my environment, and how to get better at this crazy thing called life. That is a priority for me and for that reason; I wake up earlier to make time for it.

The art of journaling and introspection is not time-consuming. It is an investment.

Before you say you cannot find time, cut out social media, Netflix, and checking emails constantly. Once you do that, I will be happy to work with you on where to find five minutes in your day for you to focus on you.

FOCUS INWARDLY

It could be a coincidence, but the more I understand myself, the more I understand others. In a year that requires leaders to be so outwardly focused, I question whether we really allowed ourselves to focus inwardly.

Why?

Because when we *do not* look inwards, we stop looking after ourselves. We burn out. We disconnect from any level of self-awareness and we fail to learn from the day to day experiences that we encounter.

True leadership is a selfless act. It requires us to do the right thing even when it is difficult and to step up when things are challenging. Most importantly, it requires us to be led by values, be self-aware, and committed to constantly learning. None of these things rely on how you act outwardly, but the measures that you take inwardly.

A leader is no good to those they lead if they are burnt out, unaligned, and unable to learn from the situations that confront them every day. In my opinion, leaders are not expected to be a finished product but to be constantly striving to be better, stronger, and smarter.

JOURNALING IS YOUR STRATEGIC ADVANTAGE

If your interpretation of journaling is, "Dear diary," think again.

Research found that journaling shows a 25% increase in performance, improves wellbeing, betters communication skills, decreases emotional distress, and improves sleep.

The above benefits are what organizations pay thousands of dollars to achieve each year through leadership courses, wellbeing strategies, and executive coaching.

Could the results they seek lie in an empty book rather than a jam-packed conference agenda?
Could what we seek be as simple as a notebook, a pen, and as little as 5 minutes a day?

Not prioritising time for journaling and introspection is not finding time to grow in your self-awareness, leadership development, and your commitment to lead yourself and others.

Journaling is simply a meeting with yourself, where you are the host and guest, the facilitator, the champion and the antagonist, all at the same time. Like any other meeting, it needs to be planned, scheduled, and prioritized to ensure it takes place and that there are tangible actions against the dedicated time.

BACKTRACK TO APRIL 2020

"The novelty of working from home is wearing off, back to back meetings are getting old, lockdowns are more serious than ever, I've just cancelled my trip to Peru, fear and anxiety are in the air, and I don't know which way is up or down."

It's all too much.

As someone who is hyper-aware of their rhythms and emotions, I felt them reach a new level. I was irrational, stressed, moving at a million hours, and not finding time to do the things that I loved. I was serving others but was losing sight of myself.

It was time to take action.

My weekly journaling routine turned into a daily routine as I accepted that I was not coping with what was happening around me and the emotions it stirred within me.

The week that I started journaling daily (five to ten minutes per day) everything changed for me.

I had clarity on my priorities.

I turned emotions into actions.

I turned experiences into knowledge (about myself and others).

I became unstuck.

I mapped out my options.

In a year where so much seemed out of my control, my journal helped me realise that I was in fact in control of how I responded. My outside world did not change (if anything it got crazier as the months went on), but my internal world changed drastically as I stepped back into the driver's seat of my life.

THE UNIVERSITY OF LIFE

My Uncle once said to me, "Andrea, you're a student in the University of Life."

I have never forgotten these words. They made me realise that I am, and always will be a student.

Whether I have five decades of experience or five hours, I am always a student. I need to be open minded and willing to receive what life teaches me, whether I like it or not. This year I learnt that I was my greatest teacher when I stopped, absorbed, and interpreted my experiences, surroundings and relationships.

Leaders are teachers, but excellent leaders are students.

NEW PAGE

If 2020 has taught me anything, it is that leadership is not glamorous. Leadership is not a step-by-step process. Leadership is messy, raw, vulnerable, and can be lonely and difficult.

Leadership requires individuals to lead themselves before others.

It requires a student mentality and an openness to giving and receiving feedback from yourself, and it requires you to be open to giving and receiving self-praising.

Leadership *isn't* a position so don't sit alongside it.

Leadership *is* a state of being, so sit in it.

Be curious, be open-minded, and be ready to lead yourself to new heights.

A MESSAGE TO MYSELF ON JANUARY 1ST, 2020:

Well, Andrea, you are in for a big year. I know you are ready to show the world who you are. You are going to achieve a lot: a new business, a podcast, a book and a promotion. You are about to embark on a journey of establishing a movement to create and promote human-centric workplaces, teaching them how to make time for introspection. It is going to be hard and your greatest tool for growth will be your ability to reflect on and navigate the challenges ahead of you.

You are stepping into a position of challenging the way things are done and challenging the way that leaders lead — promoting one's ability to lead themselves first and foremost. Some may not be ready for the concept but in time, we will see that world-class leaders—the ones who can navigate a crisis, create movements, cast a vision, and execute it—are the ones who can lead themselves with great levels of self-awareness. Reflect and learn from the moments of self-doubt, from the times when you are uncertain which way is up or down, and from the times where people cast doubt in your mind. Be a student this year (and always), because you are in for a year of learning and growth like no other. A year of stepping into leadership like you've never done before. The key to it is within — do not underestimate yourself, learn from yourself.

ABOUT THE AUTHOR

Andrea McDowell is the Founder of The Kintsugi Movement.

Kintsugi is a form of Japanese artwork whereby broken ceramics are repaired with gold, accentuating the cracks, instead of hiding them. When this philosophy is applied to our lives and workplaces, it provides great insight into healing, growth and resilience at an individual, team and organisational level. Gone are the days of trying to hide what is broken. Instead, The Kintsugi Movement focuses on embracing, empowering, and unleashing the human element.

In Andrea's chapter, she explores the value of introspection and self-awareness through the art of journaling. She also shares how journaling has developed her as a leader and individual during these times.

Andrea is a self-proclaimed human enthusiast—she loves all things people! Andrea has a Master's Degree in Business Psychology and a Bachelor's Degree in International Relations. She is a well-versed Toastmaster who has worked in the People, Culture, and Leadership space in various sectors including consultancies, government, not-for-profit, start-ups and corporates.

Andrea was born in South Africa, grew up in Australia, and recently spent five incredible years in New Zealand. She is now based in Manly, NSW, Australia where she is an avid free diver, ocean swimmer, and wannabe surfer.

Website: www.thekintsugimovement.com
LinkedIn: www.linkedin.com/in/andrea-mcdowell-b848a0130/

3

ASHISH BISARIA

LEADING FROM A DIFFERENT POINT OF VIEW

"There are events in our personal lives and our collective history that seem categorically irredeemable, moments in which the grounds for gratefulness and hope have sunk so far below the sea level of sorrow that we have ceased to believe they exist. But we have within us the consecrating capacity to rise above those moments and behold the bigger picture in all of its complexity, complementarity, and temporal sweep, and to find in what we see not illusory consolation but the truest comfort there is: that of perspective." – John Steinbeck

THE IMPORTANCE OF LEADING WITH PERSPECTIVE

The speed at which the pandemic impacted companies and employees was similar to that of a hurricane—like a catastrophic storm drawing energy from the wind, temperature of the water, and rotation of the earth. You want to evacuate, but there is no place to go.

The pandemic felt the same way. The pandemic spread human to human in close proximity, which is what we needed to avoid. But our job relied on getting people together to work and collaborate. We wanted to evacuate, but we had no place to go and keep our business functioning.

After it hit, the first question on everyone's mind was, 'Is this a pause or a great reset?' But that wasn't the right question as it assumed that there were only two possible options. For affluent people, this was a possibility. Still, for millions, the pandemic was not a pause; it was a reversal or a step back on financial growth, health, education, and opportunities. And those millions needed a quick resumption, maybe even an acceleration. To understand this moment more fully, we need a different conceptual framework or a broader perspective.

'Overview effect' is the cognitive shift that has always allowed me to contextualize and make what is or seems scary palatable, so I can step away from the "pause, reset, or acceleration" questions. It's important to view an event in its totality from the hundred-thousand-foot view first. The overview effect is reported among astronauts viewing the earth from space and seeing it through a new personal and ethical lens. It is fueled by a heightened sense of the preciousness, fragility, and interconnectedness with human life.

When viewed from an overview effect lens, the pandemic made me question ethical truths in a new and more intense way. The pandemic doesn't necessarily give us new information, but it changed my perspective and gave me an ethical repositioning. It rewired my thinking about organizations, where we are in the story, and where we go from here. It specifically changed the way I think about progress.

I am a big rock music fan, and my perspective on Eddie Van Halen has always been that he did not play the guitar; he showed the guitar what it was capable of! My role was to remind our team that we will not let the crisis lead us, but we will lead the crisis with grace. My perspective was simple; this is not a financial crisis but a humanitarian crisis.

SHOCK AND AWE: THE FIRST FEW WEEKS

It's safe to say that the speed at which this pandemic came, and the lockdowns that were ordered, took all of us by surprise. As a leader of both for-profit and non-profit organizations, we faced similar challenges in both settings: an abrupt end to the way we work (in offices), the inability to meet our customers/clients/constituents face-to-face, declining revenue streams, and fear of joblessness while dealing with personal health concerns.

In the beginning, understating the impact the pandemic was going to have on our business was gradual. Despite our office in China's COVID-19 reports back in December 2019, infections of a few Chinese staff in January 2020, and murmurs of people being infected in Europe and then the USA, I didn't expect a global shutdown. In my mind, there was no way one shuts down the world in 2020 due to a virus, given all the medical knowledge and technological capabilities that we have at our disposal.

But then March rolled in, and infections across the globe started to skyrocket. Our European offices were shut down, then our Asian offices, and eventually our last line of offices in the US closed, too. In our business model, "work from home" was limited to supporting roles, not customer management's front line role. The shutdown's impact on industries like travel and hospitality resulted in many of our clients making radical cost-cutting decisions overnight, and those cuts included doing business with us.

None of us had experienced a fast-moving pandemic. Suddenly, our employees could not be productive, our clients' businesses could not be served with status-quo processes, and long-term contracts were being canceled. With revenue disappearing, keeping the payroll going got tough. We had credit lines, but with no foreseeable resurgence in revenue, one couldn't help but worry.

Non-profit organizations that rely exclusively on donations were the first business models to be impacted by the pandemic. Our non-profit is also focused on homelessness and joblessness, the two things that were accelerated by the pandemic. Talk about a perfect storm. Funds were drying up while the demand for our services increased tenfold. The toll on employees' emotions, both from pandemic safety concerns and their job security, has been immeasurable.

As it became apparent that the pandemic was going to have a hefty toll, I was afraid, just like many others. But, as a leader, I knew that fear could not be my guide. I had to rely on professional resources I had built for decades—and that started (and ended) with gaining and providing perspective.

Still, in the beginning, I lacked clarity and direction with the pandemic and its impacts. The team was looking for a prescription from me, and I had none to give. All I knew was this: the best way through it was to help team members have hope. I could not ask scared and worried employees to give their best in times like this if there was no hope.

My message was simple: "Out of this difficulty, we will learn to do things that we can one day sit and tell our grandkids about." Life presents us with very few opportunities to do things on which legendary stories are built. This is our big moment to take a nearly unprecedented global crisis and decide how we're going to come out of it. Either way, it will be a story for the ages.

THOUGHTFUL DECISION MAKING AND A SINGLE CENTRAL VISION

Even though we were all shocked by the fast-spreading pandemic, it was my role to continue to lead an organization of people who were also scared and worried. I had to connect to my company's global workforce virtually and somehow assure them there was a successful path forward.

No, I was not the compass for the organization. A compass will point you towards the true north, but it's got no advice about the swamps, deserts, and chasms that you'll encounter along the way. If, in pursuit of your destination, you plunge ahead, heedless of obstacles, and achieve nothing more than to sink in a swamp, then what's the use of knowing the true north? Conversely, why look at the compass to show you the path? During a crisis, my role was to navigate the organization around the swamps, not just point them like a compass.

Once we got some facts about the pandemic, understood the impact office closures had on the company, and had many conversations with our customers, it was time to navigate the organization out of the crisis. It was important that the path forward was simply articulated and understood by every employee. Every decision, action, and time/money investment was made with a 'single central vision' through which all that we said and did had significance.

The single central vision was to come out of the crisis as a team without eliminating employees as much as possible, while still delivering positive business outcomes for both businesses I help lead. I understood clearly that everyone on each team is important to someone out there. These are families with interconnected lives—humanity is at stake. At no stage should decisions lead us down the path of making careless, simple choices about peoples' lives. We agreed to pursue many avenues that safeguarded our team members' health and employment.

However, the reality is that I was faced with a tough balancing act of supporting the company's financial viability while managing job security needs. The two tasks worked nearly in opposition, requiring me to manage them both while thinking large-scale about the company's ability to function. Both organizations were asking the same questions: shut down the physical work sites or keep them open? Furlough people or fire them? Voluntary pay cuts or forced pay cuts? These were just some of the opposing ideas that were being debated.

That may seem exceptionally overwhelming, but there was a way to cut down on the pressure of making the right choices, and that was through transparency in our decision making. I wanted the larger organization to know that these decisions were not easy, we were not taking the easy way out, and no, we had not forgotten the single central vision of protecting our people first.

I included as many people in solution discussions as we could. Rank and title meant nothing when debating the issues. We simultaneously combined the sense of direction and a sensitivity to reality. During decision making, war rooms, and middle-of-the-night meetings, we worked to find 'flow' in our thinking and conversations. No one was allowed to say the word 'but.' Instead, the term 'and' become our friend to help create flow. At the start of every meeting, we determined our destination and then set our sail to drive us toward the goal. We adjusted to the changing winds and currents, but all our energy was focused on navigating the deep waters efficiently and effectively. We knew that we could control only a few things, but if we aligned to the changing winds rather than forcing our way, that's how we would reach our destination. We compromised not because we were weak, but to successfully get from where we were to where we wanted to be. Persuasion was pursued with patience. Vitals were focused, and peripheral thoughts were discarded. And heated emotions were, as often as possible, met with humor.

Out of these meetings came my time-tested mantra—give people direction, not outcomes. There are a few, if not many, alternate, plausible scenarios. These scenarios have hope and a way out of the crisis at their crux, which is often all that's needed to keep hope alive among a worried workforce. I talked about our direction in stories and painted vivid pictures of our future organization to get the team inspired.

Once decisions were made, they had to be executed with steely resolve, so we relied on 'grit' to lead us forward. All this planning and decision-making came down to meeting only a few main objectives. We had to deliver our services to our clients from home. We had to move homeless people into apartments, while training them on skills remotely. We had to do this with minimal funds and limited human capital. Insufficiency demands creativity, and that, as Sun Tzu insists, requires maneuvering. That means not only planning, but also improvisation. And, in dealing with real-time improvisation, that's where our grit really came into the picture.

Daily, we were learning new things about the pandemic, our clients' expectations, and our employees' mental and physical health status. There was no way to plan even a week out. We knew we would improvise in real-time as the news came in. However, the improvisation still had to stay focused on keeping the single central vision to come out of the crisis as a team.

MY ACTIONS AND REACTIONS WERE ON FULL DISPLAY

Leaders are always under a microscope. A crisis intensifies that to an electron microscope. What I believed and, how I behaved and communicated were being watched closely. I knew the journey to the stars would get a bit more challenging and longer, but at no stage did I let people question our ability to reach our destination. During a crisis, leaders start to gravitate toward profit and loss, win or lose, market share, revenue, and other financial numbers. Heartfelt leaders begin by thinking about what impact the crisis will have on their team. While the financial health of the company is vital, you cannot have a business without people. From the pandemic onset, I was clear that we would manage this pandemic as a humanitarian crisis, not a financial crisis.

Words, behaviors, and actions had to clearly communicate "heart" before "head." Kindness had to be part of my overt acts. I made it a normal operational routine to let colleagues juggling work and family by working at home have their young children visible on video calls. No one was made to feel bad if they could not join a late evening call. We gave the benefit of the doubt to people close to us all the time. I made sure that the benefit of the doubt was extended to every team member, regardless of the situation. When mistakes happened, we talked about it publicly with positive intention. Removing fear from the room was my full-time job. I used self-deprecating humor whenever possible to help people relax.

It also required me to show vulnerability. The crisis has had emotional impacts on everyone, including me. In general, vulnerable leaders are known to inspire, come across as authentic, and build bonds that lead to increased performance—everything we need more of during a crisis. I faced uncertainty with an open heart, willing to experience all the ups and downs that came with it, not only for myself, but also for my team members. I planned to handle the realities head-on while maintaining faith and confidence that we will ultimately prevail. Being authentic, especially during the pandemic, helped build trust. Admitting mistakes, showing emotion, sharing fears, listening to learn, and not hiding behind a manufactured façade was my operating model.

One of the key things that I recommend to leaders managing a crisis is this: give your team space. The desire to be in every detail, to be in control and lead from the front, are all natural instincts. When people are stressed, they do not need a boss that dictates every detail. Trust your team. Step away and let them have breathing space to do their jobs that they've been great at for years. Yes, emotionally, they are struggling, but crowding them is the last thing you should do.

I LEARNED NEW THINGS

The reality is, there is no grand strategy for managing a crisis, particularly one of this size. The team knew, intuitively, that the way out of the crisis would evolve as we learned more. How I responded during the crisis was far more critical to the team. Did my response elicit competency, integrity, and sincerity? My response needed to be consistent, or they would not trust my response.

For example, I wrote "weekend musings," short thoughts to my team about what I learned as a leader and how they have helped me grow. For weeks at the start of the pandemic, I stopped writing. I was consumed with the idea of navigating out of the pandemic, so sharing leadership thoughts felt trite. Almost five weeks into full-blown pandemic management, a colleague shared my "lost musing." It wasn't sending the right message. In fact, it was doing just the opposite. I realized that here I was, talking about mindful leadership, the human crisis, the need to work closer as a team, but when it came to doing one of many things I had been doing every weekend, well, I sacrificed it. How could I then preach about our role as leaders when I abandoned mine?

I also learned that I should not respond to little pieces of information during a crisis but wait for all the facts. Early on, in my zeal to make a decision and appear competent, I reacted to opinions prematurely and then changed the decision as more information flowed in. So, wait until you get more facts. Base it on common sense. Common sense asks you to tether principles to decisions. Of course, the challenge is that principles are few, while decisions are many. One must see simplicities in complexity. I knew that if I were tethered to principles, they would guide my decision making.

The pandemic made me, thanks to no work travel, spend long hours reading philosophy. My "circle of concern" that typically looks after me— my family, my community, in that order, started to look out to in. "Oieiosis"—an affinity for fellow humans, made it my duty and obligation to help them. From monetary to non-monetary help, serving others became a full-time job. Buying from local small business owners and repairing the damaged shops from social unrest that got layered in 2020 allowed me to do my part to support my fellow humans.

There were many days when I felt like I was drowning in the overwhelming pain of humankind. Buried deep in water, when breathing gets difficult, I reminded myself to get a longer snorkel. My family and friends were my snorkels. Without judgment or lectures, they sat with me in silence when I needed it. I always had a shoulder to lean on and someone's outstretched arms to hug me. Exercising and running away to play golf was also my snorkel.

Finally, I had to learn to see the mountain tops and the valleys at the very same moment. Daily news at work moved between small wins and big losses. One moment, I was hopeful. The next, my hopes were dashed by some news. During crisis management, even leaders don't get to sit on mountain tops. It is on earth we live, and it is here that we must believe and act!

The pandemic has impacted millions in so many ways, and having a ringside view of the heartaches, I have to end this chapter on one thing this pandemic has brought to the surface for me: gratitude! Gratitude turns everything I have into enough.

ABOUT THE AUTHOR

For his entire career, Ashish has been guided by a simple principle: leadership is about bringing humanity to every interaction.

Born and brought up in India, Ashish embraces Eastern philosophy as the bedrock of his engagement style. Open, inquisitive, and non-judgmental, he looks at his role as a leader with a desire to make the engagement personal and memorable. Schooled in leadership from some of the best universities, including Harvard Business School, he brings the balance of structured thinking and heartfelt leadership.

Across the span of his 25-year professional career — with over a decade spent in the C-suite — Ashish has seen good and tough days at work. He has held leadership positions across seven countries, multiple industries, and many different cultural contexts, which has allowed him to connect deeply with people in ways that inspire them to follow him through thick and thin. Ashish is also on the board of a non-profit while working for a global company with 20,000 colleagues. Given how different for-profit and non-profit organization business models are, Ashish had to learn and lead them both using approaches that crossed business model boundaries.

Finally, nothing prepares you better to lead, connect, and influence than being a dad of two boys; one past his teenage days and one still a teenager. Their love and competitiveness can often be seen on social media under the hashtag #bisariaboys.

Twitter: *www.twitter.com/ashishbisaria*
LinkedIn: *www.linkedin.com/in/ashishbisaria*

4

BRENDAN DALY

THE PURPOSE OF PURPOSE

PART 1: MY PATH FROM MANAGER TO LEADER

2020 was going to be my year. December 2019 I changed careers within the same two-week period I became a father, and I had high hopes for 2020.

Why was I so bullish about 2020? All in all, I had a pretty great 2019. My wife and I completed our sailing certifications which had been a longtime goal of ours (and is a big part of our future retirement plans); I learned several new skills working with a group of private equity investors and put those to use switching careers after nearly 7 years at my prior employer; and most importantly, my wife and I welcomed our daughter to the world (yes, I read the baby books). I was winding down 2019 with a renewed energy for my career and a feeling of true happiness I'd never felt before. I knew 2020 was going to be my year.

Before my end-of-2019 career change, I'd been in roles of personnel management for over a decade. My desire for a change wasn't the result of a lack of success or advancement with my prior company. In fact, I'd been promoted 5 times in that 10-year period–all the way from Team Lead to Vice President—but still, there was something missing. My desire for something different also wasn't the result of a lack of learning; I had learned more in 2019 working with a new group of renowned business investors than I had in the prior 4 years combined. So, what was it? Why was I feeling unfulfilled in my career and wanting a change?

There are certain words often used interchangeably, but that have very different real meanings. I was encountering two sets of these at the end of 2019: father vs. dad, and manager vs. leader. In each pairing, the first title —father and manager—is relatively easy to achieve; it's the second one— dad and leader—that takes time and commitment to truly earn. In both cases, the relationship between the two words is essentially a Venn Diagram, with some overlapping area but key distinctions on either side. For father vs. dad, the overlapping area is best described as a happy child that grows to be a productive part of society. For manager vs. leader, it is an employee or team accomplishing a goal for an organization. I'm just getting started on earning my "dad badge," so I'll have to update you on that journey in another book, but the question I was trying to answer at the end of 2019 was whether I was a manager, a leader, or both.

In the first session of a management class in my MBA program, the professor opened the lesson by encouraging students to answer a simple question: what is the one thing that all leaders have in common? For the first fifteen minutes, students threw out thoughtful responses to the question: "All leaders are motivating, inspiring, passionate, good public speakers, intelligent, compassionate, etc." After every response, the professor was able to instantly provide an example of a well-known leader who didn't possess that attribute. We were all stumped; no one in a class of 50 could provide something all leaders have in common. After watching us all struggle to get the answer, the professor simply stated: "The only thing that all leaders have in common is they have followers."

I'd been a manager for over 10 years. Throughout that time, I'd seen a continual increase in the number of direct reports and teams I managed (at one point over 100 total employees) and corresponding success with those teams hitting their goals. I had direct reports, but did I have followers? My mentor once told me, "Brendan never found a problem that he couldn't address through building a process and a way to track it…" She was right, and it took me a little while to see that was both a compliment and a critique. Processes, workflows, and tasks are all critical parts of running a business, but they fall solely in the management column. Management is about planning, coordinating, and controlling to ensure objectives are met. Leadership is about motivating, inspiring, and influencing so that teams can realize their full potential to meet or exceed those objectives. As my career advanced and I took on new roles, I had to transition some of my teams to other managers. Each time, I had employees ask if they could work for me on my new teams. Hearing that always made me happy, but I never fully appreciated why. Now it's much clearer; I had reports who wanted to follow me to new teams: I had followers, I was a leader.

Vince Lombardi Jr. said, "Leaders aren't born, they are made." The circumstances by which they are made differs for everyone, for some it is an intentional focus, others necessity. My path to leadership would be best described as a slow evolution based off a positive feedback loop. I've always had a strong bias towards action, a personal commitment to quality, and somewhere along the way I realized I enjoyed teaching others and sharing knowledge. This realization came as an epiphany to me: if I could be a good leader without that knowingly being my primary focus, could I become a great leader if I committed myself to that goal?

I wanted purpose in my career, something bigger I was working toward (besides just the next promotion). I decided my new career purpose was to focus on becoming a great leader so I could enable as many others as possible to maximize their impact. I found an opportunity to start a new department (Customer Success) at a well-respected software company that had everything I was looking for: a cool product, a strong leadership team I could learn from, was well-liked by customers and employees, and ready to accelerate growth and change. I accepted an offer as Vice President of Customer Success and started my new career with purpose the first week of December 2019. I knew it: 2020 was going to be my year.

PART 2: NO PLAN SURVIVES FIRST CONTACT

I have a confession to make. I've never enjoyed reading books. It goes back to being forced to read them in high school and being told what I was supposed to take away from them (maybe Gatsby just liked yellow cars?), but throughout my adult life I've never once picked up a book to read for fun. I've always enjoyed reading online articles and magazines and learning new concepts, just not books. That statement probably seems both sacrilegious and ironic given that I'm writing it for a book, but establishing that level of trust between us is important to me, otherwise why would you believe anything else I'm sharing here?

Leaders are readers. In my journey to become a great leader, this was the statement I continued to encounter and couldn't avoid regardless how hard I tried. I was determined to succeed with my new team and new company, and I chose to turn my weakness of avoiding reading into a strength. The CEO at my new company is an avid reader and he shared several of his favorite business books with me during my onboarding. My goal was to integrate the broad perspective and experience I was able to gain by reading into my launch plans for my new Customer Success team. My research was done, my planning was done, and I was ready to embrace my purpose of becoming a great leader and launch my new department in March 2020. Then the pandemic struck.

Pandemic. The word alone is enough to cause pandemonium. It's a word most of us have heard, but few had fully experienced prior to 2020 (which is why it's making the list as Merriam-Webster's top word of 2020). Over the past 100+ years, there have been 3-4 pandemics, not including COVID-19 (most recently H1N1 in 2009). None of those pandemics had as broad of a global impact on daily life and economies as COVID-19. As Harry S. Truman said about economic trends, "It's a recession when your neighbor loses his job; it's a depression when you lose yours." Never had a public health crisis hit home for so many of us prior to 2020. Few things disrupt our ability to focus more so than uncertainty, particularly when our health or safety is at risk. For the psychology majors out there (or those of us, like me, that took one psychology class) a man by the name of Abraham Maslow made that point quite clear.

The foundational blocks of his hierarchy of needs pyramid were rocked for all of us when COVID-19 hit. Suddenly our food, water, security, safety, and even toilet paper supply were all at risk. How do you convince someone that putting in their billable hours is important when they're worried about the health of their loved ones? How long was this going to last? Could we just wait it out for a few weeks and go on as normal? How would we know when things were getting back to normal? Of all the books I recently read, there wasn't one about how to provide effective leadership during a pandemic, and at that time more than ever, businesses needed leaders not just managers.

As leaders, we can't control macro-economic or environmental events; all we can do is observe, respond, and adapt. From a business standpoint, my company was one of the lucky ones. We sell video streaming software that enables companies to live-stream at scale and were classified as an essential business. Essential business. Add that to your buzzword bingo card along with the phrases none of us knew prior to 2020: social distancing, flattening the curve, self-quarantining, herd immunity, and toilet paper rationing. Given our industry, the net impact of COVID-19 to our business was somewhat positive as it accelerated the adoption of video technology across several segments. We didn't have to rollout any furloughs or pay cuts, but that doesn't mean we didn't have our share of challenges related to the pandemic.

From the day my current company was founded 13 years ago, it was always an employee focused organization. The company embodies Peter Drucker's saying that "culture eats strategy for breakfast," and that has reflected in its success as well as rankings with several awards for top places to work. A key component of that employee focused culture was the ideation, interaction, strategizing, and alignment that took place in the office and at industry events. Overnight, we went from a 20% remote to a 100% remote workforce. We had to adapt. We immediately took the steps we read about in several business publications: send a daily email with updates from the leadership team, increase frequency of company all-hands meetings, schedule time for remote happy hours and other team building events. All these steps worked, until they didn't. We got great feedback on the daily emails for the first couple weeks, then it lost interest. We had 90%+ attendance at weekly remote trivia for the first few weeks, then it dropped to about 20% ongoing. Our happy hours on Zoom quickly devolved into another hour of talking about work. Providing a distraction from the uncertainty that was concerning us all only worked for so long.

Doesn't success solve all woes? In the first few months of the pandemic, we closed our top three largest deals in company history. We were ahead on all our pre-pandemic sales and financial goals and shared that frequently with our teams. That worked. It drove excitement and engagement, until it didn't. Why was our success in these efforts fleeting?

Focus on what you can control. It's easy to say, but what do you do when the items you can control seem inconsequential compared to world events? Record unemployment, businesses shutting down, tragic loss of life, social unrest, what kind of impact can individuals make that matters? What's the point of our work, or more accurately, what is the purpose? There's that word again: purpose. Just as identifying purpose in my career provided me with renewed energy and focus, identifying the purpose of your company will do the same for your employees.

I started my new role with the purpose to become a great leader. But why did the role exist in the first place? Why did my company want to invest in launching a Customer Success department at the end of 2019? Simply put, we wanted to get to know our customers better so we could understand why they chose us. As an employee-focused organization, we built technology that our teams believed was meaningful, cutting edge, and frankly just cool. We knew it worked well for our customers and we knew they were happy (since they kept buying more), but we didn't fully understand how it provided value for them or what they used it for. We knew which big logos used it but couldn't explain to our friends or families exactly how they used it. To maintain our position as the market leader, we knew this was something we had to remedy.

In July of 2020, we had our end of second quarter company all-hands meeting. We were in our fourth month of remote work and by this point it was starting to feel like a new normal. The short-term improvements in employee engagement from trivia, happy hour, and big bookings news had worn off. Our quarterly all-hands meetings used to be a production, the whole company would walk to a nearby event space and participate in person. Now, it was a Zoom webinar where most people's cameras were off, and they were on mute. Were people paying attention? Was this meeting engaging? We didn't really know.

In the two-weeks leading up to the all-hands meeting, the leadership team met to prepare our content. We dusted off the same PowerPoint template we'd used countless times and updated the slides with new figures: Q2 financials: on target, Q2 bookings: exceeded goals, Q2 product: we built new things. As we read through it, it all felt flat. What engagement were we providing that couldn't be sent out in a one-page PDF to the whole company? We needed something new, a new section, a new voice in the presentation: The Voice of the Customer.

Remember when I said we wanted to get to know our customers better? Despite the pandemic, we did a pretty great job of that. Our newly launched Customer Success team was holding business reviews with customers on a weekly basis and it was proving to be mutually beneficial. We were helping our customers learn about the latest and greatest features they had access to (that they were already paying for) and we were learning about how they used our software and the unique value it provided them. After meeting with the team and hearing what our customers used our software for, we selected a handful customers to spotlight in our new all hands section: The Voice of the Customer.

We save newborn babies lives. We connect people with loved ones during critical life events when they couldn't be there in person: weddings, graduations, funerals, births. We partner with companies to adapt their business models and help them avoid layoffs during the pandemic. We help keep members of the armed forces safe. And we make it so robots can watch fish on TV (yes, that's a thing).

The feedback we received from employees on our Q2 all-hands meeting was overwhelmingly positive. People connected with these stories, they saw the impact they were making, they felt a sense of purpose, and suddenly they could control a positive outcome during an increasingly uncertain time. The energy these stories gave our employees didn't fade, in fact we all wanted to know more. We shared customer stories in weekly team meetings, in Slack channels, and on companywide emails. Soon we all had a better understanding of how our products and solutions impacted the world around us. The next time we watched a presidential debate, or a spaceship launch, we knew that it was possible because of the work we did. Helping to communicate the "why" to our employees drove a stronger sense of ownership and accountability. When we had to work nights or weekends, it wasn't because we wanted to close "a big deal," it was because our customer needed to ship the next batch of NICU monitoring equipment to third world countries to decrease infant mortality. When a member of our support team was working on-call hours to support a customer's live event, it wasn't the one-time fee they paid us that mattered, it was the fact that we were able to help a trade show company pivot to remote events and keep their business open. Understanding our impact on the world gave meaning to the work our teams did. We were narrowing in on our shared purpose.

All businesses have a purpose. Our job as leaders is to identify that purpose, activate it, and ensure we live up to it every day. Identifying your company's purpose isn't easy, regardless of if you're doing it the day your company was founded or after 20 years in business. Distilling the "why" of your business' existence into 1-2 sentences takes thought, iteration, testing and time. It is a significant investment but one that pays dividends in its ability to align, motivate, and guide an organization. Many of you have heard the anecdote about John F. Kennedy's visit to NASA in 1962. The story goes something like this: during his visit, JFK saw a janitor carrying a broom. He asked the janitor what he was doing, to which the janitor replied without hesitation, "I'm helping put a man on the moon." Every role in an organization exists for a reason and once you have defined your organization's purpose, it makes it clear to employees how their role supports that purpose.

In times of crisis or uncertainty, the first thing businesses must do is avoid anything that is a good use of time. Regardless of your company's size or scale, it is easy to find a seemingly endless number of projects that are good uses of time, but the cost of settling for a good use of time is missing out on a great use of time. When the economy is strong and your industry has positive tailwinds, focusing on good uses of time instead of great ones is survivable. During more difficult times, it can be fatal. If you align your planning to your purpose, your purpose becomes the litmus test that helps you identify the great uses of time and avoid focusing only on the good.

PART 3: PROCEED WITH PURPOSE

What do Velcro, Post-It Notes, and Silly Putty have in common? They all owe their existence to a little bit of luck. We all know an example of a person or a company that succeeded in part because of happenstance. Operating with a defined purpose and focus isn't a requirement to succeed, but it certainly increases your chances. Prior to spending time defining what purpose I wanted for my career, I was still quite successful. I exceeded my objectives, received several promotions, and was well compensated. I've always had a strong work ethic and sense of accountability, but I relied on my leaders and mentors to direct me where I could drive the biggest impact. A purpose is a north star, you can navigate without it but you'll often chart a straighter path once you've found it. Furthermore, once you've helped your teams identify their purpose, you'll spend less time directing them as a manager and more time inspiring them as a leader.

So maybe your business doesn't save newborn babies lives… that's OK, not many do. Your business still drives an impact in the world, whether that's B2B or B2C. Maybe you provide a product or service that other businesses rely on to run their business. In that case, jobs exist and families are provided for thanks to the work you do. The core understanding of your purpose isn't what you do, it's the impact you provide. United Airlines' purpose statement doesn't mention anything about airplanes or flying, it simply states "Connecting People. Uniting the World." United Airlines realizes that their impact to the world isn't the act of flying, but the value a flight provides when it brings people together. That understanding of purpose goes beyond alignment and planning; it also fuels accountability and empathy. If your airline only provides flights, then it isn't that big of a deal if one is late or cancelled. If your airline's purpose is to connect people, then a cancelled flight is a missed connection, and maybe it's a connection you can't get back.

Businesses and leaders exist for the same reason: to serve the needs of their customers and shareholders. For businesses, their customers are usually external, for leaders our customers are commonly our internal teams. To serve the needs of our customers, we must first understand them. We need to interact with them, learn about what motivates them, understand the impact we have on their lives, and use that impact to codify our purpose.

This won't be the last pandemic or global economic crisis we experience. Political, environmental, and macroeconomic shifts will continue to impact our ability to plan and lead businesses. When those shifts drive positive tailwinds, our jobs are easier. The primary concerns of our teams are met, they aren't worried about furloughs or schools shutting down or whether they can visit their family members. Our priorities shift to planning the best company holiday party ever or deciding between the ping-pong table or the foosball table for our next office purchase. Those times will return and when they do, we should enjoy them and appreciate them. Tough times like we've seen in 2020 will return, too. They may not be triggered by a pandemic, it may be a natural disaster, or a large-scale global conflict, but the impact to our teams will be the same. Their core physiological and safety needs will once again feel in jeopardy, and employees will struggle to find meaning in the work they do. Our job as leaders is to be prepared with an underlying sense of purpose for ourselves and our businesses that we can use to guide meaning and impact when others are struggling to find it. Remote happy hours and trivia aren't the answer. Connectivity to our impact on the world, our purpose is.

PART 4: LEADERSHIP IS A JOURNEY, NOT A DESTINATION

Leading through a pandemic is different than managing through one, and both facets are necessary to succeed. Managing through a pandemic (or any other large-scale challenge) involves tactical shifts to ensure continuity of operations. New processes, tools, and systems may be necessary to accommodate a newly remote workforce or increased regulations for in-person events. These changes will help enable communication and coordination during stressful times, but they won't solve for the psychological challenges that large-scale uncertainty produces. Leading through a pandemic means understanding how these challenges impact our teams and providing a unifying sense of purpose to rally behind. In a sense, less is more. In this case: we don't need more remote trivia or happy hour events; we need to know how the work we do makes a difference in the world. We are all beholden to our customers, internal and external, and when we lose focus on them, we risk losing our impact and our success as a result. When things are going well, we'll all get comfortable again. We'll maintain our purpose, but at times we'll take it for granted. That's OK, as long as we remain prepared to pivot as leaders and regain focus on our purpose when challenging times return.

I wrote this chapter at the end of November 2020, 11 months into the year and 8 months into the pandemic. So far, 2020 has been my year. Personally, I've found true happiness spending time with my family and watching my daughter grow up (she's a walking machine at 11-months old). I didn't travel nearly as much as I had planned, but that turned out to be a blessing; I've lived in Colorado for almost 20 years and had barely explored my own backyard before 2020. Professionally, I've continued to grow as a leader and our business is exceeding our goals for the year. In August, I achieved one of my biggest goals when I was promoted from Vice President to COO. My work in this new role has just begun and I am humbled by the opportunity, but I am energized and motivated by my understanding of purpose. Trials and tribulations provide an opportunity to galvanize our purpose as people, leaders, and businesses, and if that's the only lesson you take away from this book or we all take away from 2020 then it's an invaluable one.

ABOUT THE AUTHOR

Brendan Daly is the Chief Operating Officer at Wowza Media Systems, the industry leading Live Video Streaming Platform.

Brendan has spent over a decade driving growth strategy, operational efficiency, and value creation through a customer centric focus at multiple technology start-ups. He received his B.S.B.A & M.B.A from the University of Denver graduating Cum Laude and is a member of the Beta Gamma Sigma business honor society.

Brendan is an avid traveler and he and his wife recently completed multiple sailing certifications together. He grew up in New Orleans, LA and now resides in Denver, CO with his wife, daughter, and dogs.

If you share a passion for partnering with customers to ensure their success and drive mutually beneficial outcomes, then feel free to connect with Brendan via LinkedIn.

LinkedIn: *www.linkedin.com/in/brendan-p-daly*

5

BRITTANY PERKINS CASTILLO

NEVER NOT WORKING: HOW TO LEAD IN AN ENVIRONMENT OF CONSTANT CRISIS

W hen I was named CEO of AshBritt, I committed to being with my team 100%. In the office, in the field, on the ground for operations – hardhat and steel-toed work boots in hand – I was determined to be there to personally direct our disaster response and recovery work in communities hard hit by hurricanes, wildfires and other disaster events.

In my first four years, I flew more than I'd ever flown, drove more highway miles than I'd ever driven. In 2016, I traveled across California, Texas, and Florida and then lived near our dumpsite in Savanah, Georgia, driving up to Charleston, South Carolina and down to St. Augustine, Florida to visit Hurricane Mathew operations. From 2017 to 2018, I was on the ground in Texas after Hurricane Harvey and ended in Sonoma County, California, managing our wildfire clean-up mission for six months. My commitment to "being with my team 100%" left my fiancé and me bouncing around the country, connecting on free weekends. And it left me buying an off-the-rack wedding dress after I stayed too long in California on a project and ran out of time to order a gown for my wedding.[1]

For my first three years as CEO, I was there. I felt connected and in control. As a leader, daily proximity gave me a pulse on my team. I could see, hear, and feel what was going on and, arguably more important, what was needed.

Then came 2020. I was pregnant, had a one-year-old, and like everyone else, was facing a pandemic. Suddenly, I went from out-front CEO to high-risk candidate and was told to isolate. My team was on the frontline, in the epicenters of the pandemic, or working around the clock at our headquarters to support our operations, and I was removed. I felt guilty, out of touch, and stressed. Then, while my company worked to plan and safely respond to hurricanes and wildfires during the pandemic, I went into labor three weeks early.

The safety of my team, the impact of the pandemic on their families, our contract performance, and new jobsite health requirements were on my mind in those first weeks after my daughter's birth. I worried about not being there at such a critical time, even though I knew I didn't have to worry. Not only did my team step up, they excelled.

From my new vantage point on *Zoom*, I had to learn to step back and lead from afar, and for a period, allow someone else to lead. I had to find my footing with the ground constantly shifting. Thankfully, I didn't have to look farther than my team for lessons in leadership during challenging times. Stepping back, even if not really by choice, I gained a new perspective on my team's success. I knew the company would be successful in managing crises in my absence because we have a culture and structure of commitment and leadership. When someone has to step back, someone else is ready and able to step in. Culture. It is as simple and complex as that.

RISING TO THE CHALLENGE

AshBritt is a U.S. leader in emergency response logistics. We help cities, counties, states, and the federal government plan, prepare, and respond to disaster events. AshBritt employees are 'second' responders – we supply food, ice, water, and housing to first responders; we clear roads to hospitals, shelters, and critical infrastructure and work alongside utility companies to clear trees so that power can be restored. We provide turnkey logistic and emergency response services such as debris removal, temporary roofing, housing reconstruction, environmental testing, and remediation.

And we have successfully provided these services to more than 600 clients, completing 400 disaster missions and responding to 60 federally declared disaster events. Hurricanes, fires, tornadoes, snowstorms, and floods: this is our expertise. Other than initial planning for a potential U.S. Ebola outbreak in 2014, we had not been previously tasked with a pandemic response.

When the coronavirus pandemic began, cities, counties, and states called upon AshBritt for help. We built and staffed field hospitals, provided around-the-clock meals to National Guardsmen and medical staff at COVID-19 testing sites, performed enhanced janitorial services, and transformed hotels into COVID-19 supported housing for the homeless. Not only did our entire team report to work, but we also worked extended hours, around the clock, seven days a week.

Like many other businesses, the pandemic required us to shift to meet our clients' needs. But unlike most companies, we are built for uncertainty and unpredictability. Our people, equipment, and supply chain not only anticipate disruption but are activated because of disruption. How AshBritt shifts from one crisis to another – wildfires (across multiple states!), tropical storms and hurricanes (30 tropical storms and 13 hurricanes in 2020!), and a global pandemic (during a major U.S. election!) – is what makes us the best in our industry. AshBritt's secret is in our culture. Four simple lessons serve as our foundation.

LESSON ONE: CULTIVATE COMMITMENT

Those who know me well know that I have two go-to statements about my team. First, eight members of AshBritt's leadership team have been together for more than 17 years, and four of them for more than 21 years. Second, team members do what it takes to get the job done.

I take pride in these facts. I believe they demonstrate our team's commitment to one another and the company. Sure, the statements also signify corporate stability and expertise in our field. Our team has done this work, together, for a long time. But what strikes me in these facts – maybe because I see it intimately, particularly during crisis – is the commitment of co-workers to each other and the company.

I ask a lot of my employees. At AshBritt, vacations are restricted four months of the year; during operations, you are expected to work seven days a week, 14-hour days; most members of our company are required to accept short-term relocations; an unofficial, internal company motto is "never not working." AshBritt's demands on one's schedule and time are matched by its demands for excellence. Governments rely on us. The stakes in disaster response are high and very public.

I require top performance in high-stress, often chaotic, always exhausting environments. AshBritt's work is hard on the employee and their family. Still, people show up. AshBritt's high employee retention is supported by three key factors.

First, AshBritt sets clear expectations on work hours and excellence. From the moment you consider a position at AshBritt, we emphasize the time commitment and lifestyle choice you make when you join our team, and we reiterate the message constantly. The directive is consistent and enforced across the board.

Second, our team supports one another. Team members do what it takes to get the job done, regardless of title, seniority, position, or the work needed. If the senior vice president needs to take a support function, he will; if he needs to stay late to get a proposal printed, assembled, and shipped, he will. If the controller needs to answer phones, she will. Our team has each other's backs. You can accomplish great things with that knowledge, that stability. And it is the only way to successfully operate during crisis if you want to ensure the health, wellness, and longevity of your team.

Third, our team is committed to the company's mission to serve communities and families in their time of need. At every level, employees are rooted in the *why* behind their tasks:

- the traffic controller is keeping co-workers and the community safe
- the finance team is paying small businesses and helping economic recovery in a disaster-impacted community
- the truck driver is picking up the debris, returning a neighborhood to safety and normalcy
- the hourly field support is handing out food, fueling first responders

When a job is grounded in value and purpose and when it is connected to the bigger picture, you can push through the hard and hectic times and better deal with frustrations and disappointments.

In late 2019 and early 2020, signs of burnout and frustration within my team, and the addition of new team members, led me to bring in a facilitator for companywide strategic planning and culture building sessions. For the first time in a decade, we sat as an organization and discussed our *why* and *how*. Through a collaborative process, we updated our mission, vision, and values. We then papered our offices and email signature lines with our refreshed focus – our *why*. Later in 2020, reflecting on the strain of the pandemic, I initiated "mission moments" during team meetings and board meetings – ensuring we begin our meetings rooted in, or simply reminded of, the why behind what we are setting out to accomplish. Likewise, I added our mission and value statement to corporate documents, particularly external documents including our subcontract and vendor agreements, outside training documents, and contractor safety training sign-in sheets.

We are a mission-centric company. Everyone who wants to do business with us should know what we stand for and that we expect them to mirror our values when working for us. Of course, I could never have anticipated what the rest of 2020 would bring when closing out the planning session in January 2020. How happy I am today that I stopped putting off strategic planning and that I allocated resources – and most importantly time – to gather the entire team for three days.[2] AshBritt's success is our team and culture. I know the extra boost from strategic planning carried each team member a bit farther and stronger in 2020.

LESSON TWO: HIERARCHY IS NOT A DIRTY WORD

Crisis management requires a clear chain of command. Hierarchy provides structure in chaos, effectuates quick action during emergencies, and provides continuity if someone becomes incapacitated. Over the last decade, many businesses moved from pyramid structures to flat teams. Certainly, there are benefits to operating flat. In fact, AshBritt runs relatively flat during non-operation periods. For our day-to-day business, we decrease management layers and strive for collaborative decision-making.

But a flat style does not work in crisis. For this reason, AshBritt maintains two organizational charts: a "non-operation" and an "operation" chart.

No two disaster events are the same and you cannot completely plan for the *when*, *how*, and *where* of a disaster, or how many disasters occur over a time period. AshBritt's operation chart provides a clear hierarchy that focuses on the roles needed for a successful response, not the specific people. We assign clear authority, accountability, and responsibility to each role. The reporting and command structure is clear, and how each role relates to the organization as a whole is clear. Then we pencil in people.

Crises evolve and priorities change. As we saw in 2020, with sickness, lack of childcare, and pandemic quarantines, people become incapacitated, be it temporarily or long term. Teams must be agile enough to adjust to changing circumstances and demands, but structured enough to make decisions, take action, and move forward, notwithstanding crisis events or incapacitated team members. With a clear hierarchy, employees know what is expected of them. Equally important, they know they can do their job and rely on their coworkers to fulfill theirs. If you are reassigned, you already have the playbook and know the players.

I deeply admire the way my team ascends to the mission at hand – supports our operations organization chart – even when it means descending in one's authority, position, title, or role. It is easy to say, "You need leadership in crisis!" or, "Create a more hierarchical structure." In practice, it's hard to get it right. In the real world, ego and prestige come into play. It may not always be comfortable, nor what someone prefers or wants, but my team accepts the roles assigned with grit, focus, and commitment to the larger team and our mission.

LESSON THREE: MAKE A DECISION

The right decision is the one that is right at the time you make it. That statement is a mantra of sorts at AshBritt. If you ask your team to step up for the mission at hand or to lead during a crisis, you need to support them and the decisions they make. They need to know you have their back.

As a company, AshBritt has to be decisive. We enter communities immediately before or after a disaster event and have to work with imperfect information and constantly changing circumstances. Delays in decision-making can directly impact health and human safety and can stress already vulnerable communities and their recovery. Delays can also unnecessarily strain employees working in taxing situations, affecting their ability to do their jobs and even their physical or mental health. These same perils of indecision faced all businesses during the pandemic.

Build a team whose judgment you trust, promote the skills needed for people to be effective leaders at your company, and cultivate a culture where employees can confidently make decisions, knowing leadership has their back. You'll weather the next crisis much stronger because of it.

LESSON FOUR: NOT EVERYTHING IN AN EMERGENCY IS AN EMERGENCY

Even in emergency response, not everything is an emergency. Distinguishing between what's urgent and what's not, between what is crucial and what is "only" important, can make or break a team. It goes directly to company culture. Successfully and routinely making this distinction is an art, one that I am still perfecting.

Leaders must be thoughtful about the expectations they set for employees' time. AshBritt requires 24/7 availability for so much of the year, which is all the more reason I must ensure my team works normal business hours when not in active operations. Because I know my team follows my example, I am learning to be more deliberate in communication around what is and what is not urgent. It is as simple as thoughtfulness of when I send an email. I started using the delayed sending feature simply so that no one feels pressure to respond to emails at night or on the weekend, which is when I find time to catch up on work, given my two babies at home. And it is as complex as conditioning employees to their ability to say no to a project or communicate that they've reached their bandwidth. I have witnessed too many times where two or three team members work excessively late (after I've gone home) to get something out the door because they were distracted by "emergency requests." More often than not, the requests came from me!

Culture matters and it is driven by intentional leadership. People burn out in crisis and 2020 has had us all living with emergencies and in an unceasing state of uncertainty. At home and work, in government and business, we are learning to live in a prolonged period of emergency response. Still, not every important item is an emergency. Learning to recognize and communicate the difference will go a long way for the benefit of the health, longevity, and performance of your team.

THE JOURNEY CONTINUES

In December 2020, I asked my team to share a word that represented their 2020 experience. I went first. My word was disconnected. Then one by one, employees shared. A theme emerged: exhausted, hectic but also grateful, engaged. How a team that works in the most volatile, strenuous environments comes out strong and ready for more after a year filled with hurricanes, fires, and a pandemic is extraordinary. It is a testament to our culture, which is directly attributed to our team. To the ones who have been there for 17 plus years – you've built this together. To the new members – you've brought in new ideas and momentum while reminding us to root back into our *why*. To the entire team – thank you for your commitment to one another and our company. To my Chairman of the Board – thank you for supporting me and for stepping in when I took two maternity leaves in two years, and thank you for building an office nursery so that I know you'll always be there when I am out, but that you also want me back!

It's funny, isn't it, that in the season I feel disconnected is when I can most appreciate how truly connected our team is, and how that's the crux of our success. From professional successes to personal success, I have the pleasure of it all weaving together. To my co-worker husband – my respect and admiration for you only grew further in 2020. And just when I thought 2020 couldn't challenge us more, the pandemic brought another twist to our family. In December, my husband, two babies, and I all contracted the coronavirus. Fortunately, and unlike millions of other families across the country, our cases were mild and we've weathered it well.

Just like work, our home has been exhausting and hectic but filled with gratitude. And just like work, I'm ready for more! To my mother – thank you for the daily reminders that not everything in parenting – every cry, bump, bruise, or restless night – is an emergency. Finally, thank you to my entire family – your humor, love, and support allow me to have two babies and be in the office and in the field, where I am most suited and happy, and from where I best lead.

---

1. I ended up with a fabulous, if not very expected, dress. Thank you, Mom, for taking my driver's license during the two days I came home for Christmas and not returning it until we did the "wedding dress thing." I am so glad we did!
2. This really should say how grateful I am that I finally listened to AshBritt's Chief of Staff, who also happens to be my husband. For years before he joined the company, Gerardo listened to me talk about our corporate strengths and weaknesses, my proud moments and my frustrations. He suggested time and again strategic planning with a facilitator. Thank you, Gerardo! You were right!

ABOUT THE AUTHOR

Brittany Perkins Castillo is the Chief Executive Officer at AshBritt Environmental, the U.S.'s leading emergency management and disaster logistics company. Brittany has led the company since 2016, overseeing major operations including: debris removal and environmental testing on 1,800+ properties following the 2017 northern California wildfires; providing shelter, food, and water to 1,000+ people and repairing and rebuilding homes after Hurricanes Harvey and Irma; building and staffing field hospitals, testing and IV therapy sites in response to the Covid-19 pandemic.

In her chapter, Brittany shares what it was like to lead a company that was responding to the pandemic and natural disasters, while pregnant and with a baby at home. She discusses the invaluable lesson of cultivating a culture of commitment and support with your team.

Brittany's background centers around crisis and logistics management. She worked in program development for a housing organization, launched the country office for an international NGO in Qatar, and built a law practice before joining AshBritt as CEO. Brittany received her B.A. from Vanderbilt University and J.D. from The University of Texas School of Law. She sits on the boards of the AshBritt Foundation, 4Girls Foundation, and The Pace Center for Girls. When not on the road, Brittany splits her time between Delray Beach, Florida and Austin, Texas, but she is most at home with her husband and two kids, ages 19 months and 5 months, in the mountains.

LinkedIn: *www.linkedin.com/in/BrittanyPCastillo*
Email: *brittany@ashbritt.com*

6

CHANDRA GUNDLAPALLI

LEAD WITH HUMILITY (NOT A HIERARCHY) WITH AN EMPOWERED CHAMPION OF CHAMPIONS OPERATING MODEL

Courageous Leadership. Lead with Humility. Build Community. Work team first, then the problem. These are the top principles I champion every day.

A courageous person will stand up for what is right, make difficult ethical decisions, and not back down when things get too hard. Cowards ignore "drag" in organizations and see only the information that agrees with their easy way out. Running from your problems is cowardly.

I grew up watching Indian cricket and played as a university captain. Cricket, like baseball in the USA, is a religion, not sport, for over 1 billion people in India.

Thirty-five years back, I woke up at 4:00 a.m. to watch the 1983 Cricket World Cup; India won the finals for the first-time, inspiring kids like me to believe that anything is possible with determination and leadership. After the World Cup win, Indian cricket had to wait almost 30 years for another achievement; winning started happening in the 2010s with two new captains, Dhoni and Virat, who changed the Indian Cricket team culture by dealing with failure, being a team player, and being the frontman. My previous 3-year experience is like the Indian Cricket journey –

management turbulence in the 2000s and courageous transformation in the 2010s.

#1 MY PRE-COVID Q3 '19

Courageous leaders challenge the coward management status quo: Indian Cricket 1983 World Cup win & management turbulence in the 2000s

In my prior role, I was part of the Dallas Fort Worth leadership council for a Fortune 500 (greater than $10B revenue) company building teams for the $100M new headquarters as Managing Director. I was very motivated with monthly new hire kick offs talking about leadership, tech talks hiring new talent, weekend volunteering, and putting company on top of family priorities while exceeding expectations in my day-to-day job. Our CEO gave me a highly selective award with stock equity in October 2018 to express deep appreciation for my contributions and a belief in my future potential. On top of this, my team received the 2018 CIO Champions award for a significant project we delivered. I felt like the Indian Cricket team winning the 1983 World Cup. The opportunity to accelerate the building of high performing teams for the company's new headquarters was one reason I accepted this role back in 2017.

In September 2019, before the COVID-19 pandemic, I started noticing unacceptable "coward management" unethical practices at this company with layoffs without any due diligence on where talent could be deployed internally in other business units. I was extremely disappointed that there was no effort from human resources to do any kind of employee strengths review to keep the dedicated top talent in other open roles. I could not stop thinking about unethical behavior in the cricket world that happened during my university days. I was rooting for new Indian cricket captain Azharuddin, who had burst onto the international cricketing arena in the 1990s, giving winning hope to the people in India, but disappointed in his cowardly role in the 2000s match-fixing scandal. I started asking myself – how do I stick with the appreciative motivation awards given to me without being vocal about coward management? At the bottom of my heart, I knew a lack of transparency on layoffs is not the leadership principle I always believed. After much internal retrospection, I had a fierce and transparent conversation on unethical practices with management. It was a sticker shock to me to realize that no one was questioning corrupt processes. I did not have many brave folks join me to hold management accountable for the unethical practices.

I had to make a tough decision to explore a new role with organizations following ethical principles. In less than a month, in October of 2019, I found an exciting opportunity as Global Vice President (GVP) at a Fortune 800 company where I could accelerate a $400M business with courageous leadership and 2000+ dedicated global technologists. In November 2019, when I tendered my resignation, I was very touched when an employee cried and my trusted network called me. My colleagues, who could not agree to unethical principles, also moved on, now with excellent roles. I see many cowards get away with corrupt practices; the industry needs a platform to voice concerns. In the cricket world, new Indian captain Dhoni took over the sacked captain's reins, changing the culture of unethical practices. This was something I would need to do as well.

#2 MY NEW ROLE IN THE COVID WORLD

Just like the Indian cricket stellar performance in the 2011 World Cup; winning TEAMS need a solid operating model on the ground.

I accepted the new GVP role to accelerate the $400M Application Modernization business, build high-performing TEAMS, and learn from the CEO trying to tackle unfunded pension obligations. To build trust & integrity in my new role, I booked my flights in February 2020 to meet my global team across India, the UK, Spain, and Brazil. I was incredibly excited about meeting my new teams in person, to kick-off a major technology event to attract top talent and to give back to Bangalore's community charity event. Then COVID hit. I had to cancel all my travel plans. I was worried about accelerating building trust & integrity with a 750+ team in India sitting 8,000 miles away without being able to meet in-person. I had to develop creative options to connect with my global organization as a trusted leader. I prioritized spending dedicated time with weekly open office hours on top of never-ending back-to-back meetings. Open virtual office hours allowed me to connect to everyone at the human level to understand their passion and challenges on the ground, and we established trust in a couple of months. I started empowering all the aspiring team members, pulling them to the priority initiatives, and making them part of the journey.

During this process, I ignored my early morning fitness routine; I had to use the morning workout time to meet my new global organization to build the needed trust to support all the major business initiatives. Parallel to this, my wife and two kiddos (12 & 10 years) started adapting to working from home and remote school learning. My ignorance on the workout took a heavy toll on me. I was rushed to the medical center ICU here in Dallas with blurred vision in the middle of the night. I did not have any pre-existing conditions. Doctors are still figuring out the root cause. They can logically advise me not to ignore workouts to reduce cholesterol levels. I am not sure if this is a COVID impact; never in my life did I expect this, as I had been healthy with a daily workout routine. While this was going on, I was shocked to learn that my parents in India got COVID. It was extremely hard for me to take care of my parents from 8,000 miles away. I am the only son which gives me responsibility for my family. I am truly fortunate to have a friend since first grade who took care of admitting my father in ICU and my mother to the hospital. I had to call a couple of family doctors in India to address hospital bed scarcity as I could not travel to India due to travel restrictions. Thank God, my parents recovered from COVID even after my father was on a ventilator. I am truly fortunate to have a strong wife and thankful for her help in caring for our two kids and me.

While I was managing my own health, my team and their families in India, were also impacted by COVID, including ICU hospitalizations and losing loved ones. We felt helpless without any proven vaccine. While I was recovering, I could not stop thinking about how my team was being impacted. At Denton Texas Medical Center in Dallas, doctors and family advised me to take it slow. My response — my personality is not wired to PAUSE as my team is struggling. I had to get back to work the next day, pulling all my strength to support my team & business growth. Personal experience taught me to connect more deeply with my team by wearing an empathy hat. I did this with dedicated weekly office hours and being there when they need me, including early mornings, late evenings, and weekends. I made it a point to call all the COVID-impacted families in my team, extending my support. And my limited bandwidth started taking a toll on my kids (weight gain, late homework), who were trying to adapt to remote learning. I prioritized my kids' activities, with 15-min schoolteachers' Zoom calls and quick power breaks (new Cricket nets in the backyard). I made it a point to remind my team members not to ignore their health. In some instances, I had to tell them to turn off their laptops.

With this personal experience, I wanted to do something to help those who were impacted by COVID. My sleep pattern changed as I thought about how families were being affected by the unforeseen pandemic with job losses. I founded a non-profit initiative #TOGETHER in June 2020, leveraging the global industry relationships I had cultivated, dedicating Sunday mornings to give back to the COVID impacted. To date, we have helped over 45 people globally by connecting them to companies for their next role.

#2.1 Need for a robust empowered operating model on the ground. How to adapt to the business priorities with agility and no additional investment?

I soon realized that open office hours without an operating model on the ground is not enough to empower my large global organization to deliver business capabilities faster. Indian Cricket team captains Dhoni & Virat had to go through a similar journey of establishing an operating model on the ground before the second World Cup win in 2011. We hear the following repeated all the time to adapt to the COVID pandemic,

- *Communication, Communication, and Communication*
- *Prioritize Employee Wellbeing*

How you execute the above depends on:

1. How agile & nimble your organization is. 99% fail due to a lack of a real, empowered workforce. Legacy structure creates problems by boxing in people.
2. The trust & integrity you establish with your workforce

promoting fierce conversations and getting to the bottom of unspoken truth to embrace different views.

More than ever, accelerating the above is needed now to mitigate the COVID impact. I've leveraged my top strengths of positivity, communication, and empathy and tapped into industry inspiration from Ford's Alan Mulally and GM's Mary Barra to create a **Courageous Conversation with Champion of Champions** operating model (Appendix).

The Champion of Champions Operating Model played a significant role in my team's rapid transition to the COVID situation. We delivered the new business opportunities without any additional budget, mitigating COVID revenue impacts:

- *Created a new COVID safety application to help the struggling cruise industry.*
- *Paused millions of mortgage payments for a top client in Brazil*
- *Built a new End User Experience practice with 24x7 support for a client in Bahrain*

Many champions in my organization stepped in to help with the new demand, going above & beyond their daily jobs without a push. In any organization, you will find 30% of aspiring individuals who always exceed expectations. The leader's responsibility is to create a platform to tap into that positive energy before losing that top talent. On top of the above business priorities, for the first time in my current company history, leading industry analysts awarded my business unit as a Major Player in Application Modernization business in October 2020. My team successfully modernized a 40-year-old legacy application in less than 4 months. These achievements are only possible with the multi-skilled cross-organization (Marketing and Workforce Strategic Planning partners) Champion of Champions Operating Model. I felt like Indian cricket winning the 2011 World Cup with a high performing team. We started the meetings with a trip report and not a status report; we talked about Indian Premier League Cricket & American Football.

I did not lose sight of the following two critical pillars in the new operating model:

- The diversity challenge is real and visible everywhere in the workplace for all minorities. It is not easy to deal with close-knit groups who are bound together by intimate social ties texting each other rather than open e-mail conversation. I am addressing this on the ground by being intentional about adding diversity in all the initiatives (hiring, all hands, promotions) and tracking quantitative progress with Key Performance Indicators every month, unlike a yearly checkbox.

- Inclusion is only a conceptual thing on paper; you will hear pin drop silence when you ask about quantitative progress. How many times you had skip-level 1:1s with the manager's manager connecting to you at the human level? I am breaking the barrier in my organization; my three levels down reach out to me directly on any concerns.

I am thrilled with the culture and technology business transformation in less than a year. I received Marquis Who's Who in America's top executive recognition for my dedication to business transformation. I achieved greater than 40% engagement and greater than 50% attrition reduction in one year, reflecting the Champion of Champions Operating Model in action. I was deeply moved to receive feedback from my team that my passion for building high-performing TEAMS was infectious and that my weekly open office hours created more trust and integrity within the organization, breaking silos.

#2.2 Addressing unethical cowardly management behavior and business revenue challenges

- On a call, one of my peers was playing the hierarchy card with my team in India without even listening to suggestions and trying to bully junior members with his title. I had to step in and nip it in the bud with a fierce conversation about creating a healthy culture. My conversation helped never to repeat the bullying hierarchy culture. As a leader, you need to step in and address the coward bullying culture. I was disappointed that other peers on the call did not step up and took the easy route of keeping quiet.

- I had to step in and educate onsite folks to build a solution partnership culture vs. order-giving culture with other global regions. The onsite person that I was coaching escalated to their manager which was an excellent opportunity for me to coach not only order-givers but also their managers to change the legacy thinking.

- With the COVID revenue impacts and client project budget cuts, the company had to make a hard decision; my business unit was not an exception. I am proud of how I have executed this, challenging the coward management status quo that I observed in my past roles. I partnered with my workforce planning team, spending 16-hour days exploring opportunities for the impacted. We were able to find a new home for the greater than 50% affected.

- Mid-year and annual performance reviews - Despite coaching all my managers to push through uncomfortable team performance conversations with accountability, I started noticing the recurring status quo of taking the easy way out. I created roundtable discussions where all the leaders now have a healthy "quantitative" debate. Now all my managers know rock stars across all the TEAMS in my organization. That was not the case six months ago.

#3 WHAT IS NEXT FOR ME?

On the positive side, the pandemic helped strengthen my resilience and focus, accelerating the foundation for my investment to "lead with humility" and courageous leadership. Currently, I am passionate about delivering a COVID project to help America get back to work safely. My team is looking forward to making a global impact with the project going live very soon. We hope for no more family hospitalizations. My wife's efforts to take our 12-year-old to practice paid off; he made it to the basketball A-team. Our 10-year-old was selected for Math Olympiad (contests & competitive homework).

As an active governing body of the local Dallas Fort Worth metroplex C-level executive summits, I am excited to promote courageous leadership and the Champion of Champions model in the industry with the partnerships I cultivated my career in the virtual world we are adopting.

#4 THREE-POINT RECAP & ADVICE

1. **Nimble Operating Model:** Create a Champion of Champions Operating Model by breaking silos to quickly adapt to unknowns, as a network with genuine, trusted relationships. Emerging technology is just an enabler; the operating model is critical for success.

2. **Lead with Compassion and Open Communications:** Focus on spending dedicated time with your workforce connecting with them at the human level. Do not jump to layoffs in pandemic situations. Focus first on solving the hard problem by wearing a courageous leadership hat. Remember, you got lucky to be in a leadership role. Be available on all the channels; your team needs you the most during unknowns.

3. **Execute the Business Purpose North Star, Making Diversity and Inclusion Real:** Help your customers with your "true" business purpose vision. Remember, the COVID pandemic is temporary. It will define your character in the long run. Trust your dedicated workforce, not the consulting firms. If your workforce is not included in the purpose, they feel apart from it.

The show must go on… Everyone is going through many life changes in the COVID world. So, humility should be at the forefront of every leader's mind. Remember trillion-dollar coach Bill Campbell's quote — "Your title makes you a manager, your people make you a leader." Lead with humility creating integrity for life; I suggest all the aspiring leaders create experiences in your organization — results will follow.

I am incredibly excited about growing the business at scale with the high performing courageous leaders I've helped to create, and with the incredible success we achieved in less than a year. In the cricket world, I am also excited about the future achievements of Indian cricket's millennial transformation – from a bunch of laggard managers to agile, ambitious courageous leaders.

#5 APPENDIX

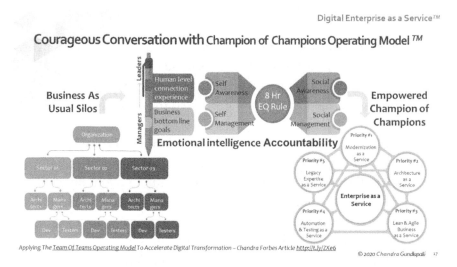

- Chandra Forbes article at http://t.ly/ZXe6
- Chandra business tech talk https://bit.ly/3cUyY8n

ABOUT THE AUTHOR

Recognized by Who's Who in America Top Executives for his dedication to the field of business culture & technology transformation, Chandra Gundlapalli excels as a Global Vice President at a Fortune 793, where he heads a $400 million business with a passion for driving business value through modernization, delivery excellence, and the high performing global Champion of Champions Operating Model™. Chandra holds multiple Enterprise as a Service™ patents with a mission to improve business friction modernization speed-to-market by >80%, leveraging his multilingual & multiculturalism (USA, LATAM, EMEA & APAC) experience.

Chandra is deeply passionate about championing Courageous Leadership with a Champion of Champions Operating Model, which is crucial for TEAM positive empowerment & agility on the ground for organizations to adapt to unforeseen circumstances quickly. Chandra is a Forbes official writer on emerging technology & the need for cultural transformations for business friction modernization. He has served in various Fortune 500 leadership roles at Charles Schwab, Thomson Reuters, Dell, and Cap Gemini in the past. Chandra learned how to build High Performing diverse TEAMS since his Masters & Bachelor of Engineering at Birla Institute of Technology and Science, and in Pilani (a top university in Asia) as a Cricket captain.

LinkedIn: *www.linkedin.com/in/chandra-gundlapalli*
Forbes: *www.bit.ly/3nY74fV*

7

CHANTÉE L. CHRISTIAN

MY BEST SHIFT

This chapter is dedicated to my parents, Elnora Christian and David Christian III. I am forever grateful for the sacrifices you made for me to have an opportunity at living the American Dream. You kept it real and taught me how to be an advocate for what is right, a fighter against what is wrong, a scholar, and most importantly, you showed me the roadmap to being a good human being! I love you both more than you could ever know!

Let me start by saying being pro-Black doesn't mean I am anti-any-other-culture and/or race. It simply means I support my community. As a Black woman, it is important for me to be an advocate and champion of my culture.

Within a year, November 2019 — November 2020, I lost five family members (grandmothers, aunt, uncle, and two cousins). It seemed like every year for seven years that my family has been hit with death. When I started this 2020 journey, I had no intention of being an advocate for social and racial justice or educating people how systemic racism has polluted our society. I just wanted to incorporate diversity, equity and inclusion (DEI) into the world I was operating in. I was reluctant to become officially 'educated' in the DEI space because I was conscious that there was no way to unknow what I knew. It is such a shift in mindset; a knowledge shift; and a physical shift because I like to think when you know better, you make a conscious choice to do better. Through that lens, I am purposeful in being intentional about the way I spent my energy, the words I used, and the way I shared my energy.

Because my father was in the Army, I was able to travel the world and see things that most wouldn't see and experience in a lifetime. As an elder millennial with baby boomers for parents, I heard discussions of racial and social injustice with varying approaches. My father was much more vocal and action-oriented, whereas my mom was less vocal, but believed in the power of the pen. Growing up observing their discussions and interactions shaped how I used my voice.

My parents would say to me, "We put all our eggs in one basket… don't drop the basket." As a child, I used to be so annoyed by that analogy and wished they would come up with a new one, but as I got older, I started to understand the concept of the fragility of an egg and how when mishandled, it can break. Now that I think of it…that was a lot of weight to put on a kid! But it was something that has rung in my head before and after every major decision I have made. I understood the weight of every action and step I made. You never know who is watching. Sometimes people think they have to make a big splash in the ocean to make a difference. So many people operate with the thought that to be impactful or to make change, they have to touch many people. I like to think that every interaction we have has the potential to have a lasting impression. I liken it to throwing a rock in a pond; it has rippling effects beyond what the eye can see. As a Black woman in a male-dominated industry, I have purposefully taken a passive approach to my advocacy. I supported organizations, efforts, and causes from behind the scenes to not outright call myself a diversity and inclusion (D&I) practitioner. Ironically, I still don't refer to myself as one; instead, I see myself as a change agent, a JEDI (Justice, Equity, Diversity, and Inclusion) Advocate, and I sprinkle it into everything I do!

Brené Brown is quoted as saying, "Daring leaders who live into their values are never silent about hard things." While that quote has always rung true for me it hit home a little differently, in 2020. I could never have predicted that the Human Interaction Lab (HIL) training I took with The National Training Laboratory (NTL) in November 2019 would be the start of my understanding of being intentional about my use of self. What do I mean by being intentional about my use of self? Well, let me start with the definition of use of self. Use of self is, "the conscious use of one's whole being in the intentional execution of one's role for effectiveness in whatever the current situation is presenting." (Auron, Jamieson & Shechtman, 2010). Before attending the HIL, I had started down a path of being intentional about *all* of my actions (verbal and non-verbal). I thought I had cracked the nut AKA life…WOW was I wrong! I realized in HIL that this was *work* and I was the *this*, and the work! Just like a car, it needs development, calibration, tuning, and regular maintenance. Developing and honing use of self is no different. It is a lifelong journey.

In HIL I was struggling personally with determining how vulnerable to be with a group of perfect strangers. If I was truly going to be open to the process that NTL provided, I needed to step into a very uncomfortable space of vulnerability. By the time they split us into our two groups (T-Groups) for the weeklong experiment, I was confident there was no way in hell I was sharing my earth-shattering news! I didn't want to take attention from the group, the work or whatever the agenda was for a pity party. I wrestled with my thoughts while also being present, but not fully present. One of the members of our group was vocal about having other things (work) going on and not being able to be *fully* present and able to do the 'work' with us. Something about that pushed me to share my big secret. On my way to the training facility, I learned that one of my grandmothers had been admitted into the hospital and had multiple strokes. Her health was touch and go. I was not trying to go tit for tat with my T-Group member; I wanted him to see that others had things going on, too, *and* still were showing up for the collective group. I shared one of the hardest things for me to say aloud, that my grandmother was dying and I felt guilt for being in a "training." My T-Group offered their support and had a bonding moment as a collective about the things that were distracting us from being *fully* present and living in the moment.

As the days continued to go by, we started to feel more like a family versus a bunch of strangers sitting in a circle. With a sense of safety, I was able to let my guard down. One of the things I was worried about most in being the only Black participant in my T-Group was that I was going to be expected to be the spokesperson for everything Black. For years, I have avoided being the Black representative. But there was a discussion that was being generated around diversity in the work environment and how it should be at all levels. At that moment, I decided to speak up; not as a Black female spokesperson, but as a Black woman in a White male-dominated industry - as me. When I finished speaking of my experiences, I recall as clear as day, someone saying, "Thank you for sharing your experience, I'll be sure to not take that on as every Black person's experience in corporate America."

I can't explain why, but I literally had a visceral reaction. My stomach was in knots and my head was spinning. I couldn't believe what I had heard. The unintentionally dismissive, discounting, minimizing and flat-out denial of the Black experience in corporate America. I responded, "You can take it how you would like, but let me offer you this. How many Black people, male or female, do you see in Fortune 500 companies as executives? How many Black people do you see in the C-Suite in any of the Fortune 500 companies?" The point of my comment was to emphasize that this wasn't just my experience, but the experience of a people who have been oppressed for years! It led me to remind my T-Group that our beloved country itself wasn't far removed from the establishment of slavery. The first Africans landed in Virginia in 1619 (400 years before the formation of our T-Group). I further reminded them that slavery was abolished in 1865, a mere 154 years ago. Along the way, and throughout the discussion, my biggest memory and most grateful experience was that I found allies in what I would call unexpected places. The biggest *shock* for me was that it took a White man to really make me step into my truth and be authentically me. He pushed me from day one of our T-Group forming to not be surface level with my responses.

In those moments I realized that 'we were doing it right'; we were interacting with each other like human beings. I was being open to the process of working on my emotional intelligence (EI), being able to read the room and know when the right time was to share my ancestors' history and how their history has impacted my current experience in the world. Through the HIL, I was able to learn how to see people for who they were and separate the impact of their words from their intention to have fruitful discussions that generated change. Fast forward to the end of that week when I received a call that essentially said things weren't looking good for my grandmother. My T-Group family supported me and allowed me to literally cry on their shoulders (anyone who knows me, knows that's not a normal thing for me), but because I didn't bottle up my feelings and shared early on, they knew why I had disappeared. They supported me through their actions. We have made conscious efforts to stay in touch and continue to do the work.

Fast forward to February 23rd, 2020, Ahmaud Arbery was murdered while jogging. A little piece of my heart broke because it was clear that a man couldn't go for a jog and look into a home being built on his route without being shot and hunted down like a wild animal. Desiring to do something impactful, I thought of several ideas yet never shared them with anyone. Then…Breonna Taylor was murdered while sleeping in her home on March 13th, 2020. I, again, had a heavy heart…and wanted to check in on my friends to ensure they were doing okay, with the back-to-back slayings of people who looked like us and could have easily been us. Coincidentally, that same weekend the East Coast of the United States announced their first city and statewide stay-at-home orders due to a novel virus known as COVID-19.

So, here we were thrust into a global pandemic and a socially tense environment at the same time. Every day that passed, I found it more difficult to sit by and keep my mouth shut, but I was still unsure what speaking up looked and felt like. I had sleepless nights because of the struggle I had within myself for what I knew was fundamentally right versus how I actually felt about not being labeled as a DEI practitioner or misunderstood as being Malcolm X Pre, pre-Mecca. Well, let me tell you. The universe or God, whomever you believe in, has a funny way of forcing your hand.

On May 25th, 2020 we watched a man cry for his mother while taking his last breath. We watched privilege and entitlement play out on TV as a White police officer kneeled on a Black man's neck, George Floyd, with his hand in his pocket and a rather smug look on his face. We heard George Floyd say countless times that he couldn't breathe. It was truly heartbreaking and devastating to witness. People around the nation and the world protested for justice for George Floyd and Breonna Taylor and police reform. Still, I didn't know what to do. I noticed that both big and small companies were coming out with statements against racism, inequities, police brutality and the like, but one company, my company, that I was expecting to hear from, was silent. For a full week, a host of companies were speaking out to include Ben and Jerry's, Amazon, Cummins, Etsy, Apple, the list went on and on!

I tried to let it go. I told myself, "*Just give them time to get their statement together, Chantée.*" I felt an overwhelming sense of obligation to my team and the company as a whole to at least ask one question: what's the company's plan to address the social and racial injustices that we are seeing play out in our backyards? Exactly one week after George Floyd's murder, I did just that, I ASKED! Five or ten years ago, I would have never asked such a question. But as a member of the leadership team and one of a few of color, the only Black female, I felt compelled.

I have such a strong belief in justice - right is right and wrong is wrong. As a person of color, I have an obligation to my ancestors, to the children in my community, and the generations that are coming behind me to say when my back was against the wall and my values weren't in alignment with an organization, I associated with values, that I didn't remain silent. I wanted to be able to sleep at night knowing when given an opportunity, I didn't sit on the sideline because the topic was hard or uncomfortable.

I wanted my team to know that they had someone in leadership that heard, saw, and empathized with them. There was a lot of discussion with some answers and possible solutions to what I thought to be a simple question. *But* I realized quickly it was not. There were days of back-and-forth emails with leadership, phone calls, and sleepless nights. These resulted in a basic email from the CEO. It lacked a true acknowledgment of what the company stood for and how action would be taken. To be fair, the email generated a discussion as to if a diversity and inclusion (D&I) committee should be established or not. The problem for me is the lack of urgency and trying to do it right. There is no right way to acknowledge. Disappointment isn't a strong enough word to describe how I felt. It was then that God or the Universe reminded me of my ideas from February and March and provided me with an opportunity to share and build my confidence. My parents raised me to be a doer, and if I wasn't willing to do, support or contribute, then I couldn't complain about what I was experiencing. As that replayed in my mind I came across a quote that said,

"Black is hard to do and be. It is African with none of the history and American with none of the privilege." I did a check-in with the Black males on my team and shared that I wanted to provide them with a space to freely express themselves. I was disappointed at the level of resistance my organization was presenting for putting out a quality statement and providing a platform for the employees to join together to have a powerful and necessary conversation around racial injustice and their shared experiences.

I was shocked and dismayed that in 2020 I had to explain to non-Black people why Black people were outraged by the countless murders of Black people at the hands of police officers. The lack of empathy for the amount of grief that Black people were and still are experiencing propelled me to step out of my comfort zone and do something! It was almost as if I could hear a voice in my head say, "Well if you can't do it for your company...where can you do it?" The answer was on Zoom! I decided to host and moderate a panel discussion with four of my fellow Black professionals from various industries to do a pulse check and provide an open and emotionally safe space for them to share their experiences during a global pandemic with heightening awareness of racial and social injustices separate from my employer.

My vision was to have a one-time event in July because I had to stand firm in my decision and block out all the external forces. Many raised their concerns around how I would market the event, how I would get panelists, how I would get the timing right because people were all 'Zoomed-Out.' I started to embody some of their concerns. So much so, that I doubted if I could get panelists and attendees. I was reminded of why it was on my heart to create a space where my fellow Black professionals could express themselves and by the grace of God, we (a few friends and I) pulled it off! The overwhelming outpouring of appreciation and shared experiences confirmed for me that this was not only the right time it was the right panelists (to whom I will forever be grateful for). It was also confirmation that non-Black people were interested in hearing the shared experiences and stories that the panelists were providing—which is exactly what I wanted to do! My goal was to provide a space where what would be considered intimate group-contained conversations could be shared openly and people of all races could relate, resonate with, and be moved to inspire action! The panel discussion was well received, attended, and most importantly, it was impactful.

I was *pushed* out of my comfort zone to host more webinars. With a little hesitation, I accepted the challenge. The slight hesitation was not because I didn't want to do it, but because of the time commitment. I was enrolled in the Strategic Diversity, Equity and Inclusion Certificate program at Georgetown University and a coaching program via iPEC, all while working my 'nine-to-five.' How does the saying go? Where there is a will there is a way? Well, I had a lot of will and God provided the way. From July to December, I hosted and moderated six monthly discussions with three to four panelists on varying topics that directly and indirectly impact the Black community.

I had to ask myself, "What am I willing to give up to show my dedication to not just my culture, but to doing the right thing?" My answer was simple: everything. I would have never said that before. Being able to explore my purpose and visualize how am I walking, breathing, and being one with my purpose has offered both clarity and the confirmation I needed. I decided that walking in purpose was more fulfilling and rewarding spiritually, emotionally, and physically than being misaligned with my beliefs and values. If that means I lose it all then I accept that. With a new charge on life, I created my own company, My Best SHIFT, LLC to be able to both coach and consult, my way.

Undoubtedly, 2020 has been filled with its countless challenges and hardships. It has also been a time of resilience and strength. While my 2020 journey has been a little bumpy, filled with emotional highs and lows, I embraced it. Having the proper language to move around the current environment of racial and social injustice has given me the confidence I didn't know I needed to be able to be an advocate for those that are marginalized. To hear my parents tell me that they are proud of me and what I have been able to accomplish this year means that I took care of the basket and protected the eggs. As a proud JEDI Advocate, I will continue to lead by helping people see that leadership starts from within.

ABOUT THE AUTHOR

Chantée Christian, CEO of My Best SHIFT, is a transformational management consultant with nearly two decades of experience in Program/Project Management, Organizational Change Management, and Strategic Planning.

As a certified facilitator, Chantée has enabled, developed, and delivered various forms of training and engagements for a range of multi-leveled staff and senior government officials. With her experience and skills, Chantée created My Best SHIFT, which empowers her to present an innovative and distinct perspective to advocacy, learning and development, leadership development, organizational change management, organization development, and program/project management. Leading by example, executing with integrity, and implementing their values in all aspects of life. My Best SHIFT strives to be relatable and walk it like they talk it!

The latest addition to what Chantée dubs as her credential alphabet soup is her Strategic Diversity, Equity, and Inclusion (DEI) Certificate from Georgetown University. This program gave her the opportunity to work with a Fortune 500 company to create an innovative DEI terminology-based training module that focused on Evolving DEI Language and Having Difficult Conversations Surrounding Race.

Website: www.MyBestSHIFT.com
Email: info@mybestshift.com
LinkedIn: www.linkedin.com/in/chanteechristian

8

DEEPAK JOSE

EPISODE 2020: IMPORTANCE OF SELF REFLECTION TO REAFFIRM, REALIZE, AND REINVENT

"Not all of us can do great things, but we can do small things with great love" -
Mother Theresa.

Well, here I go, to give a short glimpse of what felt like the longest-yet-shortest episode of my life, with great love to the best of my abilities.

I'm Deepak Jose, currently Head of Business Strategy and Advanced Analytics at Mars, Inc., living in Greater New York Metropolitan Area. Before I embark on this movie-like-memoir, I would like to thank my family, friends and colleagues who helped me get through such an unprecedented year. A special shout out to my awesome sister Deepthy, and my fiancé Subha, who has the patience of a saint.

Mind you, the stories of this episode opened a completely new narrative for the protagonist and possibly, for all other unknown invisible protagonists who fought the same fight.

I hope this chapter gives you an opportunity to take a pause, reflect, and express gratitude to all your loved ones

EP. I: A PREAMBLE TO THE PANDEMONIUM

30TH SEPTEMBER 2019

First light, munching my delicious Tostada at an Inn at Barcelona, Spain while attending an official workshop, life never seemed more satisfying. Feeling a little parched, I walked towards the cream-sugar stand to refill my coffee. I heard a scuffle behind me while I poured my coffee. I turned back and saw a person running swiftly towards a waiting car. The car sped off.

Realization dawned upon me. I quickly glanced at my table. The bag containing my laptop, passport, money, and essential documents was stolen.

Within a split second, what used to be a feeling of contentment turned to dread, helplessness, and severe stress. I blamed the Inn, the thief, myself, and mostly, the universe for making me a lab rat to test its prowess in tough luck. In that vulnerable moment, I deemed how unfortunate I was: stuck in a foreign country with no means to communicate with the locals or get help. I shook my fists at fate!

Yes. This is as bad as it gets!

Little did I know, within a few months span, what I considered as an earth-shattering problem of my tiny world would be remembered as a mere inconvenience. Brace yourself tiny world, COVID-19 is coming to put things in quite the perspective.

14TH JANUARY 2020

A colleague in China mentions a travel ban and that she is skipping the global team event.

28TH FEBRUARY 2020

Mars in-person global team meeting and then a Digital Partner Summit gets cancelled in an abundance of precaution.

12TH MARCH 2020

By mid March, the situation became dire. Greater New York City area, where I live, went into lockdown. I could see how unprepared we were to deal with such an unprecedented situation.

The pandemonium of the pandemic begins.

EP. II: AWAKENING OF THE UNCONVENTIONAL WISDOM

As days passed, the stark reality dawned upon me. I won't even be able to meet my ageing parents for the foreseeable future, coupled with the awful thought reminding me of their perfect candidature for the group deemed at risk for COVID-19. The impact on the economy is going to lead to a massive dip in job opportunities or budget cuts. Several of my friends who were working in airline, hospitality, travel and supporting services were laid off. Some others were furloughed indefinitely. For one of my friends and his family, it meant leaving the United States because of his visa status would expire in 60 days.

You could feel the blues of deteriorating mental health ubiquitously. I still remember the unshakable fear that crippled me when my sister informed me that my father turned sick in India and was admitted to a nearby hospital. I was fully aware that his neighbors tested positive for COVID-19. Traveling back to India was literally impossible as a result of the international travel ban. Even if I were able to, I wouldn't have been allowed to meet them immediately, considering the quarantine restrictions.

When you truly can't control your situation, a sense of helplessness ensues.

However, by God's grace, it was a regular fever. Nevertheless, the rising death toll due to COVID-19 included some familiar faces.

Compared to last year where travel around various continents comprised 60% of my job, I sat glued to my desktop. A rampage of thoughts was colliding within. Subsequently, I took a deep breath and thought to myself – *When you can't win the game, change the rules of the game.*

Upon introspection, I saw the silver lining among the dark clouds. The pandemic created an unprecedented opportunity for us to self-reflect and help us to align our priorities. To find light regardless of the ever-consuming negative impact around—both professionally and personally.

Aristotle, the legendary Greek philosopher, said, "Man is by nature a social animal; an individual who is unsocial naturally and not accidentally is either beneath our notice or more than human. Society is something that precedes the individual." Heretofore Aristotle might not have seen 2020 coming with its newfound rules of socializing where the word "distancing" has more weight for the survival of the said society.

My dad did not have COVID and was sent home with medication. I can't describe the amount of relief I felt. After that, video calls with my family became a daily ritual. This was the most time that I talked to my parents continuously since going off to college. My fiancé's and my favorite tradition for a getaway became spending more time in nature even though I never was an outdoor person. Bucket list items that were of lowest priority suddenly rose to the top. Yes! We finally redecorated our house, which was a long overdue task where my fiancé officially installed her art station. Some of the things we most enjoyed included hiking in the hills and National Parks of the Garden State.

My passion for my trade prompted me to upskill myself and take my productivity mantra to a whole new level. At Mars, it was a great opportunity for the team to work with the business more closely than ever before. In my current role, I am leading a global digital transformation team of data scientists and business translators focused on Advanced Analytics supporting Mars segments including Mars Wrigley (confectionary brands including M&M's, Snickers, Galaxy, Mars chocolates, Extra Gums), Pet Care (pet food brands including Pedigree, Cesar, Whiskas, Royal Canin, etc.), Mars Food (including Ben's Original, Dolmio Pasta, etc.) and the Multi-sales segment. The number of Advanced Analytics initiatives led by our team tripled since the pandemic started. We started COVID-19 impact analyses for all the key market units across the world, helping them with data-driven strategies. The dawn of this new reality equipped me to speak at 10+ industry conferences including, big e-giants like Tableau and even two podcasts.

I do have to admit that in this new journey vis-a-vis quiescence wasn't laid-back. Let's not forget the antagonist of this awakening was not solely the pandemic. However, the protagonist is just one: Humanity. A mass awakening where the sheer truth is humanity must stand together to fight this invisible battle from the pauper to the prince in their own homes.

EP. III: RE- AFFIRMATION, REALIZATION AND REINVENTION

These unconventional times fast-tracked me to Re-Affirmation, Revelation, and Reinvention. Re-affirmations relates to the affirmations which helped me to remain steadfast throughout the years and still does. Realizations relates to the new Gyan I was able to see through the rite of the pandemic. Reinventions refers to the area where I could see reinventing myself to evolve wholesomely. Of course, all three is an amalgamated experience, but the following is its essence. This helped to guide me through the pandemic as a leader and more importantly, an individual.

REAFFIRMATIONS

1. **Culture of Experimentation** – In my current role as a digital transformation leader at Mars, one facet remains quite visible. The engine of time is churning dynamically. Its direction sways by trends, economy, technology, and basic human whims. Uncertainty is a part of existence. The impulse to develop a defensive posture suits us the most, but luck favors the one who puts their energy in offense or to experiment. Success might not be the definitive outcome, but it exposes a person or a company to its best chances. We should always remember that adversity is the fuel for greatness. At Mars, even before the pandemic, we had implemented a Minimum Viable Product (MVP) culture to drive experimentation. MVP is a short-term experiment running between as small as four weeks to a maximum of twelve weeks. The objective of an MVP is to solve a small business' problem, prove out the value, and build out the business' case before scaling. The best analogy that we use is regarding moving from point A to point B — You don't need a

Ferrari but just a skateboard. This culture of experimentation came in quite handy to build out new capabilities.

2. **Progress Over Perfection** – Humans love perfection in their lives. German Philosopher Nietzsche talks about this elegantly. "Speak not of gifts or innate talents! One can name all kinds of great men who were not very gifted. But they acquired greatness, became "geniuses" …" (*Human, All Too Human, Friedrich Nietzsche*). The idea of progress explains the importance of acquiring greatness over a period. Angela Duckworth, one of my favorite authors explains genius culture in her book *Grit - power of passion and perseverance*. Everybody loves to see Usain Bolt finish 100m race in 9.58 seconds but nobody wants to see the hours he put in to perfect his mastery. In the corporate world—especially large companies—waiting for perfection is a sad reality. Many large organizations don't start any experiments until the environment is perfect. Mars is quite different from the rest of the corporate world. Mars, being a family owned organization, has associates who are typically thinking in generations and not in quarters. Invest in your small steps for a great future!

3. **Be Authentic** – Reading *True North* by Bill George reaffirmed my mantra; be authentic. Take your inspiration and passion for leadership from your own life story. Practice your values and principles with a space for unlearning. My roots are of humble beginnings from a small town in South India. Having an open mind helped me to evolve to think outside the box without the overshadowing of social conditioning. I strongly believe the very trait helped to become a better leader. The ability to unlearn, revise, and learn from all; the building blocks of being authentic. Another aspect is leading with principles and values that can enable you to make right decision during ambiguous situations like a pandemic. At Mars, all associates believe in something called the Five Principles - quality, responsibility, mutuality, efficiency, and freedom. It has helped me personally during decision making at Mars and especially during the pandemic.

REALIZATIONS:

1. **Change is normal** – The pandemic had a significant influence on consumer behavior. People are not meeting each other in person and it is putting a significant stress on everyone. We have seen significant growth in pet adoption during this time. This has had a good impact on us, and more importantly, our consumers. At Mars, we have seen our e-commerce business accelerating in all the categories. We also believe that this trend also is going to stay. Our largest customers traditionally used to deal with the e-commerce business and brick & mortar separately. Now they are going in an omnichannel route, which means they will have only one buyer. This will impact our organization and how we have organized ourselves.

2. **Importance of gratitude** – The pandemic repeatedly reminded me to have deeper appreciation towards the small things I take for granted—my close ones and I were in good health. My colleagues who tested COVID-19 positive returned healthy. A job I love dearly to support others and myself. The list really is long.

3. **Be empathetic to yourself** – Pandemic depression which included bereavement due to the deaths of beloved people and colleagues, compounded by social isolation where you have to face your vast emotions in stillness is real. A guilty conscious weighs on you for being angry for something as trivial as travel. If it were your friend, how would you empathize with them? Reminding daily, it is the way of the soulful human in me, accepting uncertainty with its plethora of emotions. So be kind to yourself. After all, we are all children trying to thrive in our adult bodies!

4. **Emotional contagion** – As a leader, and above all as a human, people should be wary of their effects on other people, whether an employee, colleague, or family member. In these highly volatile times, everyone can see the vulnerable moments people are going through. Some might be fighting depression or might even be facing financial struggles. So as fellow human, be

cautious of your aura, even to the tiniest element such as a gesture. As people are cautious about the COVID-19 contagion which could spread through contact or improper usage of masks; let's be mindful of our projections so that it won't hurt another inadvertently.

REINVENTIONS

1. **Build to Adapt** – This is a critical element for success with the Mars Digital Transformation team and especially Advanced Analytics. This has helped to customize solutions and help make changes quite easily. When we develop any digital product, we start building it in modules and always think about its reusability. Think about building capabilities like LEGO blocks. Especially since COVID-19, it has helped us tremendously to change our ability to forecast and plan our business quite remarkably. I strongly believe in moving away from a black box solution to a white box capability, which helped us further to enhance the explainability and accuracy of analytics solutions. Mars is a learning ground and—as an organization—implemented several customer solutions during the post pandemic times. It varies from our Treat Town (a virtual Halloween app to do Trick or Treating) to online pet health with online accessibility to veterinarians to several hundreds of new and innovative ideas building on the culture of innovation and experimentation. In simpler language, be like play-dough—something most kids play with. Even in the future, there will be uncertainty or even a new pandemic (God forbid. Let's hope not!). However, you should be able to adapt to every season.

2. **Mental Health Education** – is a state of physical, mental, and social well-being in which disease and infirmity are absent. One should make sure their vessel is healthy by investing in mental health in addition to physical health. Taboo around the topic does prevent people from asking for help. However, the thickening of bonds over this period helped me to remind

myself that it's alright to be vulnerable. I have started including meditation and mindfulness in my daily routine to increase my mental muscle strength.

3. **Failure is an Option** – Everyone is still fighting their own battles even as you read these lines, but my two cents to my fellow folks of humanity from my personal life whilst battling all fury is – *failure is an option*. But be wary of what you choose to fail at. To enlighten you on what I mean, let me paint you an allegory I've heard. We are all jugglers. We are all juggling various aspects of our life. It can be our personal relationships, career, family, friends and so forth. But these balls you trying to throw up in the air are made of different things. For the sake of the analogy, some are made of paper and some are made of glass. Expectations of being flawless in every domain seem utopian. So, when you juggle with all your might, make sure the ones that fall won't shatter to pieces. The wholesomeness of life relies on the battles you choose to fail at.

EP. IV: FINAL NOTE

From the beginning of history itself, man's relationship with silence and solitude is clearly seen. If you investigate all types of religion, all the holy men and women deliberately took time to be with themselves to find themselves. All those episodes of these great sages were the turning points of their life. Solitude is and always be perceived with a mixture of embroidered respect and deep apprehension. Then here I am, in the 21st century, trying to attain enlightenment in my personal bodhi tree because the COVID-19 pandemic gave all the humans in the world alike a time out. Wherever you are in the world, the coronavirus, a virion of approximately 0.06-0.125 microns, waltzed through the air and told the world to stand still.

It seems like the universe intentionally wants us to reflect on our newfound solitude for renewal. Take this as an opportunity to reflect. This will help you understand who you are as a human. Overall, the joy and sorrows of life lie in your hand and the way you handled them. As it is said in the Serenity Prayer - "God grant me the **serenity** to accept the things I cannot change, courage to change the things I can, and wisdom to know the difference."

Wishing you all a serene unconventional pandemic and I encourage you to spend some time to self-reflect to reaffirm, realize, and reinvent!

Fin.

ABOUT THE AUTHOR

Deepak Jose is a digital transformation and commercial strategy professional.

He is currently the Head of Business Strategy and Advanced Analytics at Mars. He leads analytics transformation programs for Pet Care, Mars Wrigley, Food and Multi-Sales segments to drive profitable growth for Mars and its customers. He leads a global team of data scientists and business translators driving digital transformations. Prior to Mars, Deepak was part of other global organizations like The Coca-Cola Company, ABB, and Mu Sigma in strategic roles driving business growth. He is also an Executive Data Council member at BCI Summit, based out of New York. He is an MBA from George Washington University School of Business and a mechanical engineer from NIT Calicut, India.

Deepak is originally from India and has worked and lived globally. He regularly speaks at Artificial Intelligence/Machine learning Industry conferences, including the Institute for Business Forecasting, CDAO Summit, Tableau 2020 Conference, and several analytics panel discussions and roundtables. He was a guest speaker at Hidden Layers Podcast for the world's leading experts in Advanced Analytics, and The Ivy Podcast for Digital transformation executives. Deepak is a Distinguished Toastmaster and has spoken at multiple Toastmaster conferences, Ten by Nine Nashville and Life Out Loud fundraisers.

Deepak's dream is to become a motivational speaker and to help people fight their battle of becoming better public speakers and express their true selves.

LinkedIn: *www.linkedin.com/in/deepakjose*

9

HANNAH STENNING

LEADING THROUGH THE PANDEMIC WHILE REPORTING ON IT

There is something about being in a newsroom when big news breaks.

Most days you report on the usual things: politics, sports, and too many individual human tragedies. But every now and then, something happens that changes the course of history. More often than not, you have no idea it's coming. In the Channel 9 archives, there is a tape I often think about. It's from September 10th, 2001, and it contains the most banal news stories imaginable. We had no idea that the next day's date would be forever seared into our memories.

In my career there are a handful of moments that stand out. Standing in the Today Show control room when we found out that Michael Jackson had died and throwing everything we had planned for that morning's show in the bin. The shock of Malaysian Airlines flight MH17 being shot down, which magnified as we learnt that 27 of the passengers were Australian. Being sent an unidentified link to a video in February 2019, only to watch in horror the footage of 51 people being brutally murdered in a Christchurch mosque only moments before.

There's an indescribable feeling when these moments hit. Your adrenaline is surging. You're in shock. And yet, as a leader, you have seconds to decide what to do and you don't get a second chance.

The successful leaders I've watched over the years in my time at the Today Show, 60 Minutes, and News Corp make quick decisions. They're not always the right decisions, but in the heat of the moment you have to make a call. At what point is the story or video verified enough to publish? Which reporters are you going to assign to the story? What are the angles? Who are the experts we can call on? Who is sent home to pack their bags and get on the next plane to head to the scene?

I have learnt to remain calm no matter what; keep a clear head, make a decision, don't freak out. Those are the things I'm good at.

But reporting on the pandemic has been like nothing I have ever experienced before. It wasn't a big news event that slapped us in the face. It was a slow-moving tsunami, growing bigger and closer as we watched it come for us. It's tested me and exposed my weaknesses in ways that I couldn't have imagined.

THE TEAM, BEFORE

When it comes to news gathering, things have changed dramatically since COVID-19 hit. Here are how things looked before:

For the last three years, I have been Head of Video for News Corp Australia, leading a team of video journalists who film, source, and edit footage to be published across News Corp Australia's digital websites, including Australia's biggest commercial news website, news.com.au. We work across dozens of brands but operate as one video newsroom, divided up into a News Team and a Features Team. The News Team sources breaking footage, uploading videos before digital editors know to ask for them. They manage live streams, upload requests from different newsrooms, and edit packages about the biggest events of the day. The Features Team film videos with journalists, edit in-depth explainers and animations, have fun with entertainment and royal videos — Australian's can't get enough of English royalty — and work on the topics that we know are going to be in the headlines for a while.

When news broke, we used to call out to each other across the room. Team members would collaborate to get videos done quicker. They'd say things like, "I'll make the thumbnail while you edit the video."

We had a daily stand-up meeting, where at 10am we would literally stand up from our desks, gather in a circle, and each share what we were working on and invite feedback and ideas. On Fridays, I'd buy a box of chocolates and present it to someone who had done an outstanding job that week.

I tried to build a psychologically safe environment where people weren't scared to offer feedback when they thought something could be better. I did this by being truly authentic, myself. At work, as a leader, I'm just me. As a mother of two-year-old twins, I understand that people often have things going on at home and that life can be messy. I often seek feedback and I've got the self-confidence not to feel threatened by other people's ideas being better than mine. Let's be honest, they often are.

I have built trust in my team and expect them to care about what we are doing so they give it their all without me having to micromanage.

That foundation of trust and some of those small office routines have now become invaluable.

A SLOW-MOVING TSUNAMI

January 2020 already had an apocalyptic feel to it as the largest ever bushfires ravaged our country, burning 18.6 million hectares (an area bigger than the state of Florida) and killing 34 people and over one billion animals – many indigenous and unique creatures, like the koala, are now threatened by extinction. The sky was red, and the smoke was so bad that, as I rode the bus over the Harbour Bridge at the end of my 90-minute commute, I couldn't see Sydney Harbour.

My team spent the summer sourcing footage from journalists and local residents on the ground; of people huddled on the beach or in boats when there was nowhere else to go; of koalas being saved; of some of Australia's favourite holiday destinations being burnt beyond recognition.

Our videos were watched on our websites, on Facebook and YouTube more times in January than any month before it. We had over 150 million views.

But the biggest story of 2020 was still to come.

I remember the 12th of March like it was yesterday. It was one of the last days we spent in the newsroom together as a team, and the news just kept coming. First, Tom Hanks was diagnosed with coronavirus while he was in Australia, then the NBA season was suspended after a Utah Jazz player tested positive, and finally the WHO officially declared we were dealing with a pandemic.

The waves of the tsunami that had been building for months gathered strength as we watched on in disbelief. We weren't just reporting on the news, we were living it. I'm a numbers person and I remember expressing the seriousness of what we were dealing with at our daily stand-up meeting.

"If this disease gets out and spreads to 60% of the population, then each of us will individually know at least three people who died."

I've often thought about whether highlighting this statistic with my team was alarmist, but I wanted to drill home just how important a topic we were reporting on. How science-based our communication needed to be.

That afternoon, I went straight to the small supermarket on the corner near work and joined the hordes of people stocking up because we didn't know what was ahead of us or what a lockdown could possibly look like. There's been a lot of criticism of panic buying, but as a mum of young kids I really understood the deep fear people were experiencing. My panic buying mostly consisted of a million snacks and arts and crafts material for my twins. How was I ever going to keep them occupied if we were locked up inside?!

A few days later, the supermarkets were stripped bare. Meat and toilet paper were completely gone. Rice and pasta were rationed to one packet per shopper.

The lockdown unfolded day by day. First, gatherings over 500 people were banned. Then restaurants and pubs were shut. Before we knew it, we were only allowed out of home for essential work or buying groceries. The next week, we were all sent home. My team packed up their iMac video-editing computers and left the office, all wondering how many months it would be until we returned.

LEAD YOURSELF FIRST

Now, I'm going to share some things that I hope my boss doesn't read. Seriously, Luke, if you are reading this, skip to the next section.

Ok, now that I know I'm in a safe space, here's some stuff I'm not entirely proud of.

The first three weeks at home were tough. I took my twins out of day-care and juggled them between grandparents while I tried to work.

I got so desperate to get out of the house and have half an hour to myself that I took up running. I wish I could say I spent the time running in a meditative state of mind, but I was constantly raging against the conspiracy theorists suggesting the virus was a hoax or not as bad as the flu. I would run while coming up with hypothetical arguments against them, in a rage, thinking about the healthcare workers dying in Italy and New York.

Another constant resident in my headspace was Donald Trump. It made me feel sick to think about how one man's narcissism and lack of leadership could so profoundly and absolutely destroy millions of lives. America never stood a chance with a man in charge whose ego wouldn't even allow him to listen to his country's top scientists, whose cruelty favoured division and politics over saving lives.

(Yes, I know at this point some people will accuse me of leftist media bias. But the reality is that when your job is to hear the first-person accounts from healthcare workers, scientists, and individual citizens day after day, you end up forming opinions. But those opinions don't get in the way of the verification of every story before it's published.)

Sometimes, I took lunchtime swims where I'd float in Mona Vale Basin and feel nothing but gratitude for being born in this corner of the world, where our leaders put science and human lives above all else.

In the evenings, while my husband retreated to play video games, I re-watched season after season of Gossip Girl while simultaneously doom-scrolling Twitter.

I excused my Twitter addiction because it's my job to be on top of the news, but all I was really doing was adding to the anxiety sitting in my chest. I couldn't get out of my head the capacity for human suffering, how much pain was being felt around the world, and how much more was still to come.

At night, I couldn't sleep, tossing and turning and scrolling through the horror stories in my head.

While my team were working off adrenaline, pumping out video after video, I felt like my mind was so busy racing and distracted that I barely got any work done.

A lot of my regular meetings with other parts of the business had been cancelled and I wasn't in the office to raise team morale. As a leader I felt lost. What even was my job?

SMALL THINGS THAT BUILD A TEAM

Before I share how I got out of this personal low point, I want to share three small things that have helped keep my team's positive culture alive while we've been working from home. They could be useful for any team in any industry.

1. **Daily stand-ups:** Not only did we continue our 10:00 a.m. stand-up meeting via video conference, we also introduced a 2:00 p.m. stand-up. Sometimes they only last for 5 minutes, but it's important to know what each team member is working on, giving each person a chance to speak and see each other's faces for a sense of normalcy. Which brings me to my next point.

2. **Video conference protocols:** I only ask two things. Keep your camera on and NO BACKGROUNDS. Camera on is obvious. If we're going to connect on a personal level as a team, anything like we used to in the office, we need to see each other. As for backgrounds, not only are they distracting, I also think it's important to see people in their genuine surroundings. I don't care if your house is messy or you're sitting in front of a plain white wall, there's something to be said for seeing people where they really are when you are trying to create a safe space where people can be vulnerable.

3. **Friday donation:** Prior to the pandemic, I used to give out a box of chocolates to the team member who did something outstanding that week. I'd buy them out of my own pocket because news budgets are tight. Halfway through the pandemic, when I obviously couldn't hand out chocolate in person, I changed the Friday award to a personal donation of $10 to the winner's charity of choice. It seems like a tiny thing, but it's had a huge impact. The best bit is that it gets people to share the charities close to their hearts and therefore open up in a more vulnerable way. I've seen sides of my team members I'd never seen before.

OUT THE OTHER SIDE

Ok, back to my personal struggles. The initial adjustment period may have hit me like a ton of bricks, but with hindsight I can look back and feel proud of what I achieved. And I've also done a lot of work on myself to get to a better place.

One thing I'm proud of is that while the biggest news story of our career had hit us, I was also dealing with the consequences in real life, chairing the board of a charity that previously sent therapy dogs into hospitals and nursing homes. We had to stop all visits and instantly lost our biggest income stream.

As a board, we rallied. We stood behind our staff members and didn't stand anyone down or ask for pay cuts. We organised digital therapy-dog visits, so nursing home residents could still see the dogs and feel less isolated. And we trusted our staff to find alternate revenue sources, which they did. We put financial guardrails in place, and then encouraged innovation and experimentation.

It's paid off in spades. We now have new therapy offerings, an online course, and even have slightly more money in the bank than before the pandemic began.

I handled the global crisis in the boardroom setting in a similar way to the news setting. Stay calm, keep a clear head, make a decision.

On a personal level I have done a lot of work learning to lead, myself. I went to leadership weekends and virtual courses that all reiterated the importance of slowing down and getting rid of distractions to improve performance.

I learnt how to breathe properly (it's both more complicated and simpler than it sounds) via James Nester's wonderful book *Breath*. I learnt how to meditate and visualise via Dr James Doty's incredible book *Into the Magic Shop*.

I've deleted Twitter from my phone, put time limits on all other social media apps, and I'm learning to choose my distractions wisely. My brain isn't (always) going a thousand miles an hour and I'm actively learning to be a better leader.

I've learnt that my job does have purpose, even when everyone really can look after themselves: the purpose of allowing others to do their best.

I had a moment during the recent Federal Budget night that I can't help but feel proud of. Every year in Australia, journalists are locked up for hours with the budget papers, unable to communicate with the outside world, and then released at 7:30 p.m. to file their stories. For the Budget this year, most of my team returned to the office for the event. The leaders of the News Team and Features Team had figured out what videos we needed to film and edit, and everyone knew what role they were playing. They collaborated and picked up each other's mistakes.

At 7:30 p.m., when they were released from lock-up, I only had one thing to do. I bought the pizza.

When you can trust your team to do the job, help each other when they need it, and pick up each other's mistakes, that's success.

Because when you trust someone and give them freedom to do their best, they'll want to do their best and meet the bar you set for them. They'll want to do well for you.

We went into the pandemic as a strong team, and I feel we've come out of it an even stronger one.

The trust we had built in the office has continued. The team communicates in real time in chats instead of in person, but they continue to bring their true selves to the conversations. I still see them pushing each other to improve. We've had some fun evenings playing Jackbox Party virtual games, and the team members living by themselves have reached out and supported each other when isolation got tough.

The pandemic has laid bare the importance (the literal life and death) of good leadership. So, my hope for the future is that it's not taken for granted anymore.

Good leaders are authentic, decisive, compassionate, selfless, and build trust. They put their people first.

What I've learnt most during the pandemic is that leadership skills are human skills.

We're all a work in progress. And we're all just people.

ABOUT THE AUTHOR

Hannah Stenning is Head of Video for News Corp Australia and chair of the Australian charity Delta Therapy Dogs.

In Hannah's chapter, she reveals what it was like leading a team of video journalists who were reporting on the pandemic, while also living through it.

Hannah is a journalist by trade and has previously worked as a producer on The Today Show and 60 Minutes. Those high-pressure environments inspired Hannah's passion for authentic, decisive, and compassionate leadership. Hannah thrives when her team thrives and loves helping people succeed.

Hannah lives on the Northern Beaches of Sydney, Australia, with her husband Nathan, two-year-old twin girls, and a Bernese Mountain Dog named Pumpkin.

LinkedIn: *www.linkedin.com/in/hannah-stenning-26938b16*

JAMES GILBERT

WE ARE ALL HUMAN

One morning in March of 2020, I received a text message from my mother that read, "Son, do you guys have toilet paper in your cold storage?"

Now, we don't live close. It's not the norm for her to check up on my family's stock of personal hygiene items. I responded, "No we don't. Why?" Amongst all the necessities of life — food, water, first aid kits, even generators — we were covered.

Toilet paper? Nope!

She promptly responded, "Watch the news, and get yourself some quick."

I offered the obligatory, "Okay, Mom. Will do," and, thinking nothing of it, I made my way to the grocery store. To my disbelief, shelves and shelves of food, toilet paper, and other essential items were completely out of stock. Five minutes searching for toilet paper on my phone, and it became apparent that every site — Amazon, Walmart, CVS, Walgreens, Target, Costco, etc. — was going to offer me the same "out of stock" greeting.

My wife and I had to laugh when I told her the news that night. We had maybe three weeks' worth of the apparently valuable commodity left.

So, I did what anyone would do when faced with this dire situation. I ordered a bidet and a whole lot of wipes. You see, I have four kids — one of which is still figuring out why he can't poop in a pull-up.

Enough said.

As my two bidets and a few weeks' worth of wipes made their way to our house, I found myself watching social media. I saw videos of the country being asked to shut down. I saw people in grocery stores, fighting over TP like it was the newest Xbox on Black Friday. All kinds of home-made hand sanitizer tricks popped up on Pinterest, but even the liquor stores were wiped clean. What I witnessed on social media the rest of that week — like so many of us — made my heart sink. How quickly we had turned against each other when it came to wiping our butts.

All kidding aside, I was astonished. Why had it come to such drastic measures? Still, in the back of my head and heart was hope — hope that we could rally together and help one another. Lending a helping hand has always been a part of who I am.

The reason? My mother.

With five siblings, you could say I come from a fairly large family. We had a fearsome mother who — along with the help of my grandparents and aunt — raised us all as a single mom while working as a home care nurse. We knew at times what it was like to do without, but we also knew what it was like to be prepared. My mother worked hard, and that attribute was solidly engraved in our souls. More important than that was what our souls were made of. An upbringing around God was at the center of our home and hearts. And we practiced a simple principle that anyone — whether or not they believe in God — can live by: treat others the way you want to be treated. This was in our bones. I may not have always lived it, but it was something I strived for every day.

THE FALLACY OF LEADERSHIP AND CARING

I kept this principle in the front of my mind, as I progressed in my career. With my leaders, I took note of things I didn't like, things I would do differently, and things that I loved. Without fail, when a conflict arrived that I had to lead through — or one that I failed at leading through —

those words always came back to me. Treat others the way you want to be treated. This grew in my mind and heart, and it's become part of my leadership style.

Oh, I heard all the noise from other leaders: "You can't be their friends," they said. "You want their respect? You can't always be the nice guy."

You name it, I heard it. I remember some of my own leaders using these very same tactics on me, and guess what? I hated it. Those aren't the leaders I try to emulate or the ones that I call for advice. The leaders that cared — that were human with me — I speak to often. They have helped me make big decisions in my life. Leaders like Tom Love (alias), who taught me a deeply empathetic and peaceful way to manage. He was always calm, always kind, and always the humblest person in the room. There are obviously many others I learned from, but no one that showed compassion and empathy quite like Tom. He was my friend, but I knew clearly where the line between boss and friend was. I respected that. I respected him, and I always followed him into our battles.

This necessity of empathy, compassion, respect, and humility became even more evident as the middle of March 2020 made its way into our lives. Close to seven months prior — in October of 2019 — our start-up, CloudCherry, was acquired by Cisco. The doors of opportunity were opened to me at Cisco, but the big enterprise life was something I've lived before. I enjoyed the work, but the part that I really love is helping things grow into their potential from very little. I knew my initial contract was short at Cisco. They'd given me until March (pre-pandemic) to decide whether I'd stay or leave. I was working well with the team and truly enjoyed the culture. When the pandemic hit, Cisco's already stellar HR stepped up even more, helping us every step of the way. I was unsure of what to do. In March, that indecisiveness moved the position that had been open for me prior to the pandemic to a N/A status.

I was worried. I knew what was happening in the world and — like so many — I was scared I'd end up without a job. Yet another incredible leader — my previous CEO at CloudCherry — helped guide me through this. He'd always led with empathy. I remember when we all got news of the acquisition. Almost anyone who's experienced it can attest to the strange combination of emotion that hits you — excited but bummed. We wanted to ride-out it with our team. We had created such an amazing global culture, and we'd grown to truly care for one another. Our CEO worked out incredible, completely unheard-of packages for us all. For those that didn't have a permanent option at Cisco, he offered his personal help in landing a new gig. Think that happens by accident? No, he built that culture from the start.

SEEING OTHERS THROUGH A DIFFERENT LENS

I recall — early on in the CloudCherry days — a struggle of alignment between the U.S. side of the business and the global side. Certain areas of the business were run out of their origins in India, while we knew the growth of the company's success had to hinge on the U.S. operations. Cultural differences were evident. Our CEO put together a company retreat to India, giving his entire team the chance to embrace their traditions, holidays, food, and culture. He knew this would help break down barriers.

It's experiences like these that helped us develop a better sense of understanding — a deeper connection to humanity that is bigger than ourselves, and the opportunity to witness another lesson from my childhood in action: choose to see others for who they can become.

Cultural and religious differences, political views, and even race do play a role in who we are — for good or bad, but none of those differences change our ability to treat others like we want to be treated and — in doing so — also see the best potential version of each other. It's a choice.

WE CAN'T PREDICT THE FUTURE, BUT WE CAN LEAD PEOPLE INTO A BETTER ONE

Back in March 2020, as I was searching for a job, my previous CEO referred me to a new start-up that needed some help. What initially began as just some consulting on my part quickly developed into an offer. There wasn't some miraculous playbook I had that others did not. This had everything to do with the relationships I had fostered and developed over time. In a world of ever-deepening differences, these relationships are still what makes it go 'round.

Shortly after I joined my newest adventure, I began hearing about more and more of lay-offs and people losing their jobs. Our struggling world needed leaders who chose compassion more than ever. I saw hundreds of LinkedIn posts about Zoom calls and images of teams that were used to meeting in person instead confined to squares on a screen. It tested a skill set they never knew they'd need. People grew frustrated — not united. They felt alone — not connected. They felt lost. I watched businesses operate in a new way for contactless delivery, contactless banking, contactless grocery delivery, a whole lot of contactless-ness.

I watched my own team — stepping into new roles, struggling with family and children, or — for those who've been weathering this "new normal" on their own — dealing with the soul-crushing feeling of isolation. With the pandemic's progression, I really had no idea when I'd get to meet them in person. This meant my virtual leadership had to seriously step up. It had to go above and beyond anything my in-person leadership had ever been. That was uncharted territory for me.

With this new terrain came more reflection. I remembered another practice that had impacted me as a young leader: mindfulness training. It's a practice I'm continually trying to master, as it's no secret I'm beyond passionate about certain things. And remembering that training made me more intensely aware of the vulnerable situation each person on my team was in. I began listening more closely. I made it a habit to always have my video on in meetings, so they could see that I was there — that I was present, and that they could rely on me. I also began leveraging a heavy dose of emojis in my communication. As insignificant as a change like that might seem, it made a difference. It offered a small but potent dose of human emotion to our interactions and opened a path to the kind of expression this pandemic had made difficult to share. Oh sure, we'd seen virtual coffee talks, wine tasting seminars, and online events, but, we hadn't witnessed enough actual transparency in how leaders — and the people they lead — were dealing with their individual breaking points, all now too close to the surface.

As a leader, the general expectation in our culture is to be "professionally" emotionless — come what may. It's the deepest desire of so many to reach the top of their field — to finally get to that position. And I find it fascinating to watch the realization that happens once they've arrived and learn what the view's really like from up there. The simple fact is — even CEOs are human. Board members are human. Advisors are human. And, unless you've figured out a way to run every role at a company on AI, well guess what? It's run by humans — each with a breaking point, each with a desire to be respected, appreciated, and loved.

Unfortunately, all that humanity has an ugly side. Too often during the pandemic, compassion and respect have been hard to find. From the beginning, the media gave us a view of people tearing each other apart — fighting over masks vs no-masks, right vs left, police vs. BLM, white vs black. We saw murders, cities destroyed, people defamed, and businesses go bankrupt. The days of respectfully disagreeing became a thing of the past. We became almost addicts to reacting. People hid behind their screens, and we grew accustomed to a virtual world that normalized saying or acting any which way you please. You could drop an ugly comment or two and scroll on down, choosing not to see the consequences. We were humans behind an avatar behind a screen. Fear spiked. And that fear too often overpowered the desire to speak up, when minorities needed voices to be heard. Toxic division was — and still is — changing everything we thought we knew about our communities.

WHO SHAKES THE JAR?

Have you ever heard the scenario of the red ant and the black ant? If you take the two and place them in a jar, they'll work together. However, if you shake the jar with them inside and dump them out, they will fight to the death. So the question becomes: who's shaking the jar?

With our new work-from-home existence, the line between work and home-life disintegrated. Hours blended together, and we became workaholics without even realizing it. Zoom calls and multi-tasking filled our days. And single moms and dads were asked to homeschool their kids, while working full-time. Offices were being created in people's beds, closets, porches — you name it. Small businesses were being shut down. Unemployment skyrocketed. Riots impacted residential and business areas.

Yet, we still heard leaders say, "Hey, you need to be on video." "You don't have any more PTO to use." "We don't offer child-care reimbursement." "We can't afford to give you equipment for your home office."

Let me ask an honest question: Is this what matters to *you*, as a leader? Is it worth it to *you* to forget the humanity part of all this — to reject the idea of perhaps offering a day-off, no strings attached? Are demands on already overworked single moms or dads worth the pay off? To quote the Mandalorian, "This is NOT the way."

The person on the other side of that text, social media post, grocery aisle, or phone call is a human — just like you. They, like you, have beliefs and values that run deep — that are an inseparable part of who they *are*. Are their beliefs different than yours? Ok. Let them be different. Differences make us better. Differences make us stronger. They are the red ant; you are the black. We can live peacefully in the same jar — without allowing the world to shake us into the ugliest version of ourselves. Even at the highest level, small decisions can be made to have a short-term and long-term impact, and we have choices here. It should be simple: choose to be better than that.

WOULD YOU MANAGE YOURSELF THAT WAY?

This is where we, as leaders, have to step-up. It's time we stop letting past processes, agenda-driven social causes, checkboxes of diversity — all part of the old "norm"— dictate whether or not we're humane to those around us. If you're expecting a playbook or a consultant to come in and give you ground-breaking advice, good luck. It's time to embrace a simpler approach: treat others the way you want to be treated. Put aside your differences, and lead people with the kind of compassion they desperately need right now. Your people need to be seen and heard. They need to be loved and appreciated and respected. They need the opportunity to grow — even if that means outgrowing you. They need leaders like the ones you wish you had.

The pandemic brought the worst out in some of us. We lost our way as a society the moment we started fighting — literally — over what wipes our butts. And we lost our way as humans when we weren't willing to respect each other's differences. Those months exposed weaknesses and made it glaringly apparent where we need to do better. We needed to put a little extra on our shoulders, so that others could take a break — to give time off for mental health (corporate policy be damned), and to offer employees a safe place to express their views, without risk of retaliation. We needed to remember the human side through all of it. Like my friends in India taught me, we needed to *celebrate* differences — to see beyond color or race, political views, and gender stereotypes. We needed to give our employees a reason to experience this crazy life with us, and to try — always — to see them for who they can become.

Now, if you feel I'm preaching from the rooftop here, rest assured I've been drinking my own Kool-Aid. I've hired people for their talent, not to check a box. I've tried to put potential ahead of bullet-points on a resume. It just so happens that most of my team in the US is made up of women — not due to some prearranged intention to create more diversity within our organization, but because they were the right people for the jobs. And together we've built a culture of true out-of-the-box thinking, ownership, respect, vulnerability, and of completing work with integrity. The result? A team that was genuinely empowered to — not just think outside the box — but to throw the box out entirely. They took ownership in understanding our product better and more quickly applied their skills. I mean — they built an entire campaign around how The Bachelorette relates to CRM and had me — for the first time in my career — talking about *love* on LinkedIn!

As a leader, I'm not willing to believe the fallacy that you can't truly care about your people without compromise, that you can't befriend them for fear of not being respected. And — for that — I may one day be seen as a leader who pushed the status quo and completely failed. If that day comes, I will gladly accept it. I'll know that I never compromised my integrity or my forever-engrained determination to both treat people the way I'd like to be treated, and to see them for what they have the potential to become.

These core principles are in all of us. After all, we're all human. We all have a breaking point — vulnerabilities we've witnessed in each other throughout the pandemic. So, maybe ask yourself: did you take time to see the beauty and the even greater potential in those who actually broke? Did you encourage them to see it for themselves? Did you help the mother of four — a stressed out, homeschooling survivor behind the name on a Zoom avatar — see the light at the end of all this? These are the kind of questions every leader should be asking — in every team meeting, every executive discussion, and every interaction with another person. We are all human, and we can all be better.

ABOUT THE AUTHOR

James Gilbert is first and foremost a family man. He is a husband to a wonderful wife and father to four children based out of Salt Lake City, UT. He and his family love exploring new places, camping, hiking, kayaking, and they love to be outdoors.

James is known as a living inspiration. He went blind before and during his years attending college while he waited for the miracle of a transplant, requiring him to change course in his life. While on track to become a civil engineer, James learned to love numbers. He soon found himself in roles that spanned sales, operations, and marketing. He learned that being agile with his skills didn't mean being agile with his soul or character.

James learned to play the piano when he was blind; learning by ear. This is a process he credits to helping him hone his marketing strengths. With over 15 years of experience, he is now known as a marketing game-changer and leads the Global Marketing Team at CRMNext, the leading enterprise CRM solution provider for financial services. James loves to leverage data and new technologies to strengthen and maintain the human element in all aspects of the consumer experience.

James is also an active author for Forbes, a leader in the PEAK online marketing community among others, an international speaker, podcast host, advisory board member, consultant, and local and national non-profit volunteer.

LinkedIn: *www.linkedin.com/in/jrgilbert1*

JAMES JACKSON, III

A LEADERSHIP ABILITY UNVEILED

"I Am Not What Happened to Me. I Am What I Choose to Become."

The year of the pandemic transformed me into a different leader from what I was the year before. I have had imposter syndrome for the last several years, while growing an organization with an important platform in a small community.

Inside, I was not always confident in my leadership, although it may have shown on the outside. As the Founder and Executive Director of the Utah Black Chamber, the year 2020 showed me that I had no choice but to lead as if I had the ability, even when I did not necessarily have the right experience and confidence. My comfort zone has never been this stretched. I have grown into my leadership skin and fully owned the success of taking the organization through such a challenging time. The main reason for the success was realizing a very powerful leadership ability and it has grown to become one of my biggest strengths. It is the ability to connect with people. Here, I will share the five skills I have learned about connecting with people.

#1: CONNECTING BEGINS WITH HUMILITY

"Started From the Bottom, Now We're Here"

Have you ever agreed to do something only because you knew you would have the support, but then the support left after you committed? What did you do? When I founded the Utah Black Chamber in 2009, I had no experience or knowledge about starting and leading a chamber of commerce. I was encouraged by a church and family friend to lead a Black chamber that was failing. The leader was not leading with the vision he tried to instill in them after flying out of state to learn how a Black chamber operates. I hated to see another Black organization in Utah fail, and I followed up with him to see how I could help. He asked if I would be willing to step up and lead. I did not know what he saw, but he sold me on the idea and I agreed to the mission. While he was not able to commit to mentoring me as he originally planned, I eventually found my path by learning to build a network and gained various mentors and people who wanted to help. I remained humble, continued to ask questions, and followed through with everything they asked me to do. I was always open and honest with them. I never shied away from saying, "I don't know." I still do not today. I paid attention, learned, attended events held by other chambers, and spent several years working to build the right leadership.

The Utah Black Chamber has since become one of the most influential all-volunteer-based organizations in the state of Utah. I have gained exceptional leaders residing on the board, and we have built partnerships within the local Black community, other civic organizations, and government. Many have elected to join our chamber because we are the 'Fun Chamber,' not just because we are the Black chamber who values partnerships, people, and progress. People enjoy working with us because we engage with everyone and allow people to be their authentic selves, no matter their background. We always follow through and get things done.

#2: CONNECTORS SUSTAIN BY BEING AVAILABLE

Leaders Pause, Pivot, and Persevere

At the beginning of the pandemic, my biggest concern was keeping the Utah Black Chamber operating and serving the community through it. Most businesses closed down, and those that remained in operation were not nearly at full capacity and struggled to survive. We paused renewing memberships, and stopped working to get new members. We were not holding any events either. Everything just came to a standstill. I felt like I failed as a leader. I tried to give myself some leniency. How many leaders have been through a pandemic? There is really nothing that can be done, right? No matter how much I tried to reason with myself, it did not sit right with me. How can the chamber continue to make the impact, inspire businesses, help them sustain, and keep them growing? This is new territory for me. We tried online events as well as sharing resources and funding opportunities as often as we could, but I just did not feel it was enough. Black-owned businesses were closing their doors at an alarming rate, and as an organization that is supposed to support them, I could not find the strategy to do what I felt we should have been doing.

As a Black chamber in a homogenous community, we have to be creative. I like to think big and dream big. However, in a time of uncertainty, thinking big and dreaming big came with many asterisks; *post COVID-19, *with no COVID-19, *if we can have big crowds again, etc. Leaders want to create, motivate, and elevate everything around them. During this pandemic, I had a hard time dreaming as big as I wanted to, as I felt too discouraged by uncertainty.

In February, just before the pandemic, the Black Chamber announced that it would build a Black Success Center — an economic development hub for Utah's Black community - a facility for businesses, business professionals, and community could come for connection and personal and professional development. It was more of a vision than an actual plan, but after sharing this with other leaders within and outside the chamber, I knew that once this project was completed, it would transform not only the Black community, but also the state of Utah.

Then the second pandemic hit the nation; racial injustice. Because of the Black Chamber's growing influence, we were at the forefront of the Black Lives Matter movement in Utah. People contacted us to contribute, support, and provide assistance for our membership, our community, and us. As a result, we were able to develop many programs, including building a smaller pilot of the Black Success Center. As the economy began to reopen, we began planning for not only a grand opening of the pilot Black Success Center, but also the launch of the Chamber's Northern Utah Chapter. It was less than a weeks later when new COVID-19 restrictions arrived due to a surge of cases, and we had to cancel our whole event. We had all the precautions in place, including a smaller crowd and online streaming, but it was not enough to comply with the new restrictions. Therefore, we had to pivot towards promoting it in a different way. This is how the pandemic has challenged leaders. While we feel like it kills our dreams and hopes of what we want to do, we have to continue to be resilient. We have to pivot from our original plan, have a plan B and C, and sometimes, things will just have to be put on hold and we will have to just stay in the moment, focusing on what we can just do in the moment.

Following the countrywide protests sparked by the murder of George Floyd, the chamber leadership constantly communicated with the media and engaged in the community. In the beginning, we quickly became busy, and there was no way I would be able to be the face of the organization all the time, as I have before. Our team stepped in and stepped up, without asking, and without hesitation. People and organizations I never considered connecting with the chamber were contacting us. The Utah Black Chamber experienced massive growth the next several months. We made more of an impact in the community than we ever have in a given year, and expect to do so much more in 2021 than we have ever done in the previous ten years serving the community. I did not realize how prepared we were to handle the attention and the responsibility. Yet, we handled it with poise and resiliency, and continued to strengthen our platform. I was leading discussions with local leaders and media every week for several weeks. While it was exhausting, I realized we were the voice for those that did not have a voice. It was our responsibility to educate and navigate the community around us, while leading, protecting, and providing resources for the local Black community. Because of this, I have learned to embrace my influence and platform and lead with a new and stronger vision.

It was a lot to adjust to and embrace. Handling the virtual meetings and phone calls from morning to dusk was exhausting. The isolated feeling I appreciated as an introvert was no longer available. However, because my fiancé, Michelle, and I, were working from home, we became better pet owners and took our dog, Max, for walks in the morning before starting our workday. It was not only healthy for Max, but for us, too. Walking around the neighborhood got us out of the house and we got some fresh air. We got some time to talk to one another, vent, and exhale—whatever we needed to do to get the day going and support each other. Having a partner by my side was immeasurably helpful. I could not imagine dealing with this alone. She took breaks on our back patio to break away from her office space, and I learned to take advantage of that part of our house as well to take a break whenever I had a chance. Even when there was so much to do, I knew if I did not take a timeout, I would break. I just needed to disconnect from everything and take a breath. Those breaks have become part of my normal routine. Sometimes, I do not even go back to my desk, but take my laptop to another area of the house to have a fresh work environment. That helped stimulate my mind and got my working juices flowing to help me get through the rest of the day.

#3: CONNECTING IS NOT A PERSONALITY

It is an Ability That Can Be Learned

We all connect with people in some way. Most of us connect unconsciously, without realizing how powerful the ability to connect with people can increase our influence. As someone who grew up naturally quiet, I communicated more by listening than speaking. I enjoyed the conversations more when I spoke less. Most people enjoyed speaking with me, because they felt listened to and valued by me just listening. As I grew my ability to connect with people, I have never needed to apply for an opportunity. People reached out to me or I had an existing relationship with them. Moreover, when I wondered if I have had the right talents, skills, or abilities for a role, I found that my skills for connecting and leadership were more highly valued by my employers. The rest, they believed, could be taught. For example, in a role I had a few years ago at a bank as a Community Reinvestment Act (CRA) analyst, my manager said to me that he could teach me everything about CRA, and how our bank managed the program, but what he most valued was how I connected to the community. He saw it as something that could not be taught. I realize now, I learned this ability over time by observing mentors and leaders who influenced me. Although most of it came naturally as a product of my personality, everything I possess can be taught, and when learned and applied, one can have a transformative influence in your leadership ability.

#4: BRIDGE-BUILDING IS A CONNECTOR'S SUPERPOWER

Listen to Understand, Rather Than Listen to Respond

As the pandemic lasted longer than projected and the racial and social justice movement grew during an election year, the discussions around the issues grew more intense and more divisive. It was frustrating to witness and engage in these conversations. It caused emotional stress and issues for many, and others retaliated with verbal abuse or even other forms of abuse. I had never seen our country so divided and simply could not comprehend why people overlooked the police brutality and racial injustice, and there were so many mixed messages on how to manage COVID-19. Leaders who have influenced my life have had passion, vision, common sense, logic, and integrity. Many who have been the most influential during this pandemic, whether good or bad, have had none of that; no common sense, logic, nor integrity. Rather, they would use whatever data, information, or story they could find to support their agenda. It did not matter who it affected or where it came from. Sometimes, they just used the headline of an article and not even read the whole thing. Alternatively, they would change the meaning of people's interviews around to meet their agenda. This method transcended to their followers and the more it spread, the more divided we became. It was almost like another pandemic.

After seeing this, I took it upon myself to bring some understanding, using my ability to connect with people. I stepped out of my comfort zone, embracing my leadership role in the community, and put on my social justice hat. In every interview I had, I shared the theme, 'listen to understand, rather than listen to respond.' I wanted to help people gain an understanding of learning from both perspectives. I started hosting weekly virtually meetings. The first one, over ninety people attended: from family members, chamber members and partners, and people from all over the community. Even a local police chief discovered the meeting and attended.

We had a great discussion, and I felt I was making an impact. The police chief shared in the discussion a few times and felt the conversation was progressive; he invited other police chiefs to attend the next meeting. I had eight police chiefs attend and over sixty other people from across the country. I gave the police chiefs the forum, and I just moderated the call. The chiefs were understanding and the community was understanding too. It was so gratifying to see the impact of just a couple of these meetings. From there, I met with a few of those police chiefs individually, and have been working since to build the bridge between law enforcement and community.

#5: FINDING COMMON GROUND

Learn to Walk in Other's Shoes

Imagine two islands apart from each other. Each island represents a different perspective from the other. One is left and the other is right. One is conservative and the other is liberal. One wants masks mandated, and the other does not. The only way these islands can be connected is with a bridge. However, instead of a bridge, a wall is up, blocking the view to the other island, or better yet, there is a drawbridge, and the bridge is up, blocking our views and our perspective is not reaching the other island. We need to bring down the bridge, in order to connect the islands. The bridge is common ground, where each side can come together; share their own view in a civil discussion. What we hope to come out of that discussion is not only an understanding of one another's view, but hope to find solutions to the issues that divide us today. It will not be the vision of one island or the other, but a new vision.

People are emotional beings. We are not principally logical, but emotional. To understand how to connect with people emotionally, we need to understand that we do not see the world as it is. We see the world as we are, and we are all different. There is something different that has happened to the average adult that changes the way they see things and that difference is called 'conditioning.' In our upbringing, we have been influenced by whom we follow, listen to, watch, and learn from. That influence has conditioned us to believe a certain way. While we all have good intentions, our perspectives can at times disagree with others and sometimes offend them. This is why it is important to find common ground. Listening is the main skill I possess that helps me find common ground. This is the most critical skill that we, as a nation, are struggling with today. We have to listen intently and with sincere curiosity. We cannot be arrogant enough to assume we understand their view. Brené Brown defines connection as the energy that exists between people when they feel seen, valued, and heard. When you make that connection, people become more open to share. The more you allow them to be open, the more they share and the better understanding you gain. John Maxwell says, "People don't care how much you know, until they know how much you care." Do not share what you know. Do not try to control the conversation. Leading is caring. Leading is humility. Leading is listening. Leading is being sincerely curious. Leading this way will bring down the barriers of arrogance and indifference and form bridges.

It does not matter what level of leadership you possess. At any level in our lives, we have some level of influence. It does not matter your position, title, or income level. In fact, the chamber leadership is greater than me in any or all of those levels; position, title, or income. However, I understand my ability to connect with others, and that is what attracts the people who help grow my vision within the chamber and raise my influence in the community. Knowing this for yourself, becoming more intentional in connecting with people and finding common ground, you'll uncover relationships and opportunities to elevate your life as well. Yes, knowledge, experience, talent, and skills are important, but your influence and ability to connect with people will be the primary vehicle to take you to your destiny. Leading during the pandemic was tough. I never want to go through this experience again. However, I am grateful for the journey, the growth, and the realization of how this powerful ability can change your life.

ABOUT THE AUTHOR

James Jackson, III serves as the Supplier Diversity Program Manager as Zions Bancorporation, where he is responsible for building relationships with capable diverse suppliers who provide goods and services across the enterprise. Mr. Jackson has worked in various areas of the financial industry for nearly twenty years, and found his passion serving and building his community.

In conjunction with his role at the bank, Mr. Jackson serves on several boards of directors, and is the founder of the Utah Black Chamber. Since its inception in 2009, the Chamber has grown to not only serve Black-owned small businesses in Utah but has also become the premier organization connecting and engaging Utah's Black community and building bridges for inclusion.

From the Chamber, he started—or helped start—several other programs to elevate Utah's diverse community, including Living Color Utah and the Utah Diversity Career Fair. Various communities, government, and corporations seek his guidance on topics of diversity and inclusion. Such inquiries prompted him to start his own business, J3 Motivation, focused on providing coaching, training, teaching leadership, and organizational development.

As a native of Utah, he is committed to the social and economic growth of the Black and overall diverse community.

LinkedIn: *www.linkedin.com/in/jamesjacksoniii*
Website: *www.jamesjackson3.com*
Utah Black Chamber of Commerce:
    www.utahblackchamber.com

JENNIFER ANGLIN
MANUFACTURED RESULTS

One cannot predict how people will react to a pandemic. As a leader, I have experienced the good, bad, and ugly during this period where we are all figuring out what our new normal is. I can even say humbly that all my actions were not always the best choice or could have been carried out differently. They were all the above because no college education, leadership book, or even good past leadership experience could have prepared me for how to be an always strong, calm leader amidst a pandemic. This past year has been full of learning and understanding.

I have always been referred to as a "planner." I was the kid who knew her class schedule before school started and always had her clothes set out the night before. I knew what I wanted in life and had a plan to accomplish my goals. My natural planning tendencies have had me going-on thirty since I was eight years-old. This planning complex fit me well early on and led me to pursue a career in business. I found my niche in supply chain management. I loved the complexity of putting the pieces of a process together and figuring out how to get from points A-to-Z. I am a "super planner," and my brain is constantly analyzing and re-analyzing the plans, backup plans, and backups to the backup plans, much to the chagrin of my sleep schedule. I have worked for the same large, well-known consumer packaged goods company for almost ten years, and knowing the industry well, I thought I had a good handle on the curve-balls that could be thrown my way. My planning skills continued to develop throughout my early to mid-career years in supply chain roles, but such skills were truly tested and taken to another level when I started my next challenge as the first female Operations Manager at one of the world's largest consumer packaged goods manufacturing plants in two major events – one local, another world-wide.

I moved to Arkansas 2 years ago for my first leadership role in manu-facturing. I left a corporate leadership role in Atlanta, Georgia, where I was in a Senior Manager position leading a multi-tiered, large-scale supply planning team, supporting seven manufacturing sites across the United States and Canada. What I loved most about transitioning to Operations Manager was being a part of where the action was in making consumer packaged goods. I have always been fascinated by the manufacturing process and was excited to engage with employees on the manufacturing floor. Having grown up in a family business, I appreciated the community feel of working in a plant. This sense of community took time to develop given that site never had a female leader, and here I was from corporate, blonde, and relatively young! The best part of my day was my daily rounds in seeing what was happening and engaging with employees.

After 3 months at the plant, I found myself preparing a 450-person manufacturing plant for a 1,000-year flood. In previous job roles, I supported the manufacturing plants in the path of Mother Nature: weather events and unplanned events including fires and water main breaks. Now I had to do the heavy lifting of how to keep operating a large plant facing a 1,000-year flood when main highways were shut down, causing severe personnel absences and supply-chain logistics issues. The planning skills kicked in, and the plant made it through rather unscathed. While in Arkansas, I have also learned how to develop contingency plans for tornados, power outages, hailstorms, labor strikes, material shortages, safety events, etc. With this contingency planning experience, I had the "Yeah, I got this. I'm a super planner" mentality.

Having lived in more than eight different states, I found Arkansas to be a place that naturally socially distances. Given the state only has three to four major cities, the population is fairly spread out. Fortunately, being located near the middle of the contiguous 48-states, Arkansas was one of the last states to be impacted by COVID-19; however, it was disconcerting watching the spread of the virus coming at you from all sides. I think back to February when I would be talking to family in Ohio and listening to them commenting on the virus and impacts it was having on their communities. In all reality, I thought it was more of a northern thing since the flu typically has such a bigger impact in colder climates. The idea of the virus impacting Arkansas did not really hit me until mid-March. I had gone for an annual doctor visit and decided to take the entire day off to run errands. My doctor and I had discussed the virus, but neither of us were overly concerned at the time and briefly discussed how people could stay healthy. After the visit, I met one of my colleagues to pick up a few masks from her, "just in case" I needed them. Her mom was making them for healthcare workers and she offered them to me for work. Then, I took a trip to Target. While in the store, my husband called to say "Hi" and told me about what he had heard that morning on the news regarding the virus. I just so happened to be in the cleaning products aisle and thought to myself, being a mild germaphobe, that if this virus became a big deal, I had better stock up on some things because I sure as heck was not going to run out of cleaning supplies. I was glad I did because that weekend was when President Trump declared the coronavirus pandemic a national emergency.

The weekend the pandemic was declared a national emergency was when my planning and leadership skills were applied far beyond what I was ready for. The chaos began. I was getting a grasp of what a pandemic meant and how it would affect my team and myself. A pandemic was not in my contingency plans. I had no idea where to start with comprehending what would ensue. A reality check hit hard! My leadership team at the plant immediately convened as that announcement was made about the national emergency. I was responsible for developing the site's pandemic response plan. The response plan ended up being over fifty pages of comprehensive details outlining contacts, processes, essential equipment, priority lists, and escalations. That weekend was the start of the exhaustion that would be felt for the balance of 2020 and myself questioning my confidence and abilities as a leader. As tiresome as this early planning was, it was necessary as the cards were going to stack up against me quickly as a leader with finding a way to keep a 24/7, 362-day operation running that employs nearly 450 people and keep each of them safe.

With the announcement of the national emergency, my corporate capabilities, support teams, and corporate based employees stopped traveling and worked remotely from home. That meant my team had no onsite support for new product trials, troubleshooting, equipment installations, and operations excellence. As such, I had to take on additional tasks all while trying to increase production output to meet the increased consumer demands for our manufactured products. This also meant my corporate counterparts had more time to focus all their attention on the manufacturing locations, which turned into yet another task of handholding that landed squarely on my desk.

On the other side of the spectrum, employees immediately started asking if I was going to shut down the plant due the coronavirus, with concerns that landed in two competing camps – compensation and health. Most employees were concerned about how to support their families if the facility did shut down. Some of the employees at the plant were part of those categorized by the CDC as high risk. I also faced challenges with employees not able to come to work due to a lack of childcare when schools shut down. Then there were the outspoken employees who were outliers that thought I should shut the plant down. They were not ones whom you could reason with or explain my response plans to. They tried their best to intimidate me and made comments that we did not care as leaders – that the company valued profit over people. Their reaction was disheartening; knowing most of the people graciously thanked me for keeping the plant running. What those few outliers lacked compassion for was that I had tough days every day and I had to make decisions that were best for most of the work force and longevity of the business.

It was hard for me, knowing that most of the world transitioned to working remotely and from home, when my manufacturing team and I had to show up every day. There is no ability to work from home in manufacturing or to stay safe at home. The show must go on and my facility was considered one of essential manufacturing. In my family, I was the only one leaving our house each day. Fortunately, my husband was able to work from home, which our three dogs absolutely loved and now expect! I felt uneasy, being the only one leaving each day, as I knew if either of us got sick, it would be me being exposed to the germs from coronavirus and bringing those germs home. I also started to miss my previous role in Atlanta, knowing that had I not taken this role in Arkansas I could have been working from home. This was tough to wrestle with emotionally because I knew coming to Arkansas was the best move for our family's well-being and career growth, but I was struggling to stay upbeat about it. I was tired all the time, both physically and emotionally. Thankfully, my husband could relate as he was a leader on his employer's COVID-19 committee, and we would discuss best practices. The frustrating part was not knowing when all this would end or what was going to happen. Summer is always the busiest time of the year for our plant and this was going to be an even longer, hotter summer in Arkansas.

My site remained COVID-19 free and it was almost the end of June! As a leader, I felt like my site was in a good position. I missed the normalcy of my daily rounds on the production floor. I could not talk to employees as I used to, or fist bump to celebrate when we had a good production day. There were days I did not make it on the production floor due to meetings about COVID-19 and picking up work that I no longer had outside support for. I knew I was doing several things right after hearing stories from other company sites and organizations on how the virus affected them with sending employees home or shutting down their facility, but it sure did not feel like it. My team wanted to high-five as we made it halfway through the busy summer with no incidents, but knew it was only a matter of time. By this time, our employees were aware of and comfortable with our pandemic response plan and benefits that were available to them in these unprecedented times. Employees even helped me come up with solutions to the close contact ways in which they could work together differently. They understood how to work safely and became problem solvers.

That gut punch moment of an employee at our site testing positive happened two days before I was to go on my first vacation of the year and a week before Independence Day. This was not ideal, but I was glad to be there to lead the team, as I knew this situation was going to be challenging. As soon as the site was notified, our leadership team met to enact our response plan and how to best communicate to the employees. We had a good plan, but there was no way to stop the chaos from erupting! Following the first employee testing positive, the plan was for leaders to meet with all employees and crews to update them on what was happening at the plant and our path forward. We had talking points that covered what happened, what we were doing to keep employees safe, cleaning of equipment, and future plans. As I gave my update in these meetings, some employees responded with disrespect, yelling at me, blaming me for what happened, and claiming that I did not care about them. I know it was hard for them to hear what happened and they were scared, but my patience and strength were being tested. I remember asking God to give me the strength to get through this day as I took the heat. I reflected on many quotes about leadership and being the calm in midst of the storm. In that moment, I had to embody that. I managed to keep my intention and purpose. I also knew that as a female leader in a site that was not accustomed to female leadership, I would be judged even more harshly if I did not keep my composure. I refused to have the reputation of being the one who acted high on emotion. After the crew meetings, two of my colleagues even made a comment about how well I did in delivering the message and not letting the upset employees set me off and take over the meeting.

Throughout the summer and into fall, the unsolicited advice from other company employees outside the plant began to take its toll. I was doing everything imaginable as a leader to be persistent, compassionate, and creative to keep equipment running. However, others did not see this daily effort. Summer vacation and time off had been non-existent, thus adding to the continued mental and physical exhaustion. I would be on conference calls, get emails and phone calls saying. "Oh, you should do this," or "Did you think about that?" or "Why would you do that?" I realize and appreciate that people are truly trying to help, but until they walked a mile in my shoes and experienced what our team/employees were, it was hard to know. Even the most experienced leaders in our company and industry were learning. Relationships changed with colleagues who I relied on due to their lack of understanding and humility for what the site was facing. There were days I was beyond exhausted from the pressure applied by corporate to keep running due to continued high, unforecasted customer demand and managing the constant concerns from our work force. Every day we faced labor shortages due to direct and indirect impacts of COVID-19. I worked more hours than before and adjusted my schedule to be available to address employee concerns as our facility operated 24/7 with four shifts that did not rotate. I even learned to operate production equipment! Everyone in manufacturing faced similar challenges. There are no one-size fits-all approach, especially to a situation that is full of emotions that are constantly changing. The best I could do as a leader was draw on my experience, lean on my team, and keep a "boots on the ground" approach to knowing what I could do best as a leader. I found that being present and, in the moment, gave me the best sense of leadership capability and the agility to quickly pivot on decisions based on the information I had at the time.

My brain is still on overdrive. I am worn out as this pandemic continues. However, the amazing thing and source of a huge sense of accomplishment is that even with all the adversity that we faced and conquered this year, my facility had the greatest production year ever. I am beyond proud to be a leader in all of this! I tell people to thank fellow friends and colleagues in manufacturing. Check in on them to say "Hi" and see how they are. They are also the ones on the frontlines putting in the extra time to make and restock the shelves with products that families use daily. One of my hopes for the future is that people are appreciative of those in manufacturing and understand how vital they are to our economy. Manufacturing is a tough industry and supports many families in our country. This industry is often overlooked as it is not glamourous or seen as cool.

This experience has taught me that regardless of policies, rules, regulations, facts, and opinions, the most important thing is to be human. Manufacturing, and the leaders who support those organizations, must continue to be flexible and thrive in the wake of these tough events. It has been no easy task at our plant to keep 450 people safe, healthy, and motivated. I overcame more challenges than I could have ever imagined as a leader and faced constant change. The challenges continue to come, but each day I show up to do the best I can for our people and the plant. No matter how hard it was, I am thankful for my manufacturing team and constant family support. I especially could not have gotten through this without my husband's encouragement and dogs to come home to. Even through the exhaustion and the tears, I know that I am a good leader. Every day I strive to lead in the best way I can. I will continue to be the coach, teacher, student, and cheerleader. I will continue to be resilient and never give up, as I know this experience will open doors to continued leadership opportunities.

ABOUT THE AUTHOR

Jennifer Anglin is a supply chain and operations leader with over ten years of experience across multiple consumer packaged goods. Her peers and colleagues know her as a super planner and organization queen. She has a passion for developing talent and building high performance teams. Jen has a proven track record of improving relationships between manufacturing leadership and corporate support groups.

In Jen's chapter, she talks about being the first female Operations Leader at the production plant she currently works at and how her exceptional planning skills were challenged in a way that she would never have imagined. In her leadership role, Jen has been able to draw on her experience of leading multi-tier supply chain teams of over twenty employees and manufacturing teams of 400+ employees. Her career journey has enabled her to live in eight states, her favorite of which is South Carolina. Her experiences, both personal and professionally, have fueled her desire to be a quick and continuous learner.

Jen received her B.S. from Michigan State University and M.B.A from Louisiana State University.

Outside of work, she enjoys running and spending time with her husband, Ed. They have three dogs; Simba, Kuba, and Tulsa.

LinkedIn: *www.linkedin.com/in/jennifer-a-b2713a14/*
Email: *Jennifer.anglin@live.com*

13

KASIA HEIN-PETERS

LEADING WITH SCIENCE (AND SOMETIMES WITH SCIENCE-FICTION)

My life was very well organized in January 2020, if not a little hectic due to newly expanded job responsibilities – adding medical affairs and market access to my already busy job.

Travels, a few strategic projects, change management, and a new marketing strategy process kept me occupied. In my personal life, I continued complaining to my husband that I did not see him often enough and I tried to talk to my elderly parents in Poland at least once a week. My weekends were filled with hiking and nature photography and reading about Japanese history to better understand the culture of Terumo, our parent company. I had a very busy, but stable and fulfilled life, which seems so distant now.

My awareness about the pandemic grew slowly. I was always tuned to health news and noticed the first media reports about the new respiratory virus in China sometime in early January. Viruses jump from animals to humans all the time, so it did not register as anything out of the ordinary to me. Then human-to-human transmission was confirmed, though the number of cases was still low. At that time, it felt like it would be similar to previous SARS and MERS epidemics, with rather regional spread, which were scary but finally relatively easy to contain. Nothing to worry about in a world full of microbes. The United States felt safe and far away from the problem.

My trip to Japan in mid-January was interesting but uneventful, and I came back just before Wuhan was locked down on January 23. I was still watching the evolving situation in China like a sci-fi movie, unreal and in a galaxy far, far away. Then first papers were published about the virus transmissibility and the severity of symptoms, and the extremely high age-related mortality rate. These were early red flags that indicated that the new disease was much more infectious and serious than the flu, which kills up to 600,000 people every year. Then outbreaks occurred on a few cruise ships and in Italy, and news came from the Centers for Disease Control and Prevention (CDC) that their tests were faulty, so they only tested a few hundred people in February. At that moment, I knew that 2020 would be a rough year and that we may have lost our first battle with the virus in the United States. The community spread was already occurring, and we missed the opportunity to contain the epidemic at the early stages of single cases and small clusters. My anxiety increased, and I canceled the Caribbean cruise that my husband and I had planned for late March. Three weeks later, the cruise industry put all cruises on hold.

At the company level, we were already mapping our supply routes, refreshing business continuity procedures, and responding to customers' requests for more inventory. At that time, I oversaw corporate communications, among other responsibilities, and had extensive experience in crisis management from my previous work in the pharma and vaccine industry – so it became my job to lead the crisis response team. Our company realized that we needed to act quickly to protect our associates (the company's employees) from the coronavirus as much as possible, as there was already more community spread than detected by testing, which continued to be in short supply. Fortunately, as a medical device company, we had a small group of physicians and scientists who could sort through emerging science and help to design new ways of working, even before the public health authorities in Colorado issued a stay-at-home order. In retrospect, turning to science was the best decision that we made at the beginning of the pandemic. We followed the official public health recommendations but also were able to adjust their policies to our specific situation, especially protecting associates who could not work from home.

As a medical device manufacturer, our obligation is to continue production and ensure that our products reach customers without delay, as they were needed for various treatments and blood donations around the world. Manufacturing associates, engineers developing new devices, and scientists conducting laboratory studies were unable to work from home, so we had to create a safe environment for them. Mandates for masks, physical distancing whenever possible, and enhanced hygiene on campus were introduced. Personal protective equipment (PPE) was provided and associates were divided into groups with limited movements between buildings. During the recent wave, sample testing started on campus to identify associates who tested positive. Thanks to all these measures, outbreaks were avoided on campus and only isolated COVID-19 cases and small asymptomatic clusters were observed in the recent months when the numbers of new infections in the community reached a new high.

The first months of the pandemic felt like an endless workstream consisting of catching up with newly developing science about the virus, its transmission, disease symptoms and severity, checking news and public health websites for information about evolving situation around the globe, and following changing public health recommendations. Communications had to be developed frequently, informing associates about the changing work practices, testing availability, and addressing customers' concerns. Workdays became long, and almost all other projects were put on a back burner. I do not even recall what else was happening at that time. And if it wasn't enough, the level of confusion and disinformation spread by fringe political groups (and later by mainstream politicians) resulted in anxiety and a feeling of uncertainty among our associates. The fear was palpable, and I had difficulty in addressing pressures coming from all sides, including the disappointments related to non-COVID-19 projects' delays. I burnt out at that time but could not take time off due to the intensity and amount of workload. Finally, a few trips with my husband, long hikes in my favorite canyons, and creative hobbies helped me to get back on track.

We express a narrow range of behaviors when we are anxious – flight, fight, or freeze. We realized that in our company, many associates were "freezing" – sitting tight and waiting for what will happen or for the pandemic to be over, and deferring decisions to the headquarters. Initially, it was exacerbated by the natural tendency to centralize decision-making during a crisis. The behavior was understandable but counterproductive, and in late March, we realized that we could not function in a continuous crisis mode. Instead, we had to organize ourselves for longer-term challenges, develop new operating mechanisms for the fiscal year 2020, and identify business opportunities while addressing the pandemic-related challenges. The leadership needed to ensure that we were all aligned around the same strategy, and that the decision-making process was decentralized so there would be no bottlenecks between groups and layers of the organization. The purpose was to create an easily adaptable, leaner culture that would allow the company to move back and forth between lockdowns and reopenings, adjust production, quickly digitalize customer communication and keep the supply chains open. Our team focused on science again to dispel some myths and conspiracy theories and to help associates understand the rationale and evidence behind measures implemented on campus. The communication team started regular, short virtual sessions to address associates' questions. We covered popular topics, such as viral transmission, social distancing, masks, hygiene and virus survival on surfaces, testing, mental health during the COVID-19 pandemic, COVID-19 vaccines, and many other. For some associates, we became the main source of facts about COVID-19, and the attendance during our sessions grew to several hundred.

To evolve our COVID-19 response team, we found inspiration in the Star Trek series and announced the creation of the United Federation of Planets (UFP) – a team of teams organized to address specific issues, which worked like sovereign planets, managing their affairs and making their own decisions related to their "planetary operations." Some of the "planets" were addressing manufacturing productivity and supply chain, associates' health, blood shortages, new ways of working, new business opportunities, regional issues, and others. Associates were included in these cross-functional "planets" based not only on their functions but also skills and interests. The UFP Cabinet was set up to support the UFP President (our CEO), decide on the strategy and operating mechanisms, and make decisions affecting the entire Federation (the company). Meetings were set with a regular cadence to exchange information and address new issues, which were emerging frequently. This new team was not only much more efficient and closer to the front line but also allowed us to mobilize the right resources in case of new challenges and opportunities. It was also a little fun introduced to an otherwise very somber situation.

Like in many other medical device companies, some of our business declined during the pandemic due to cancellations and delays of elective surgical procedures. Elective procedures, as opposed to emergency procedures, are typically not lifesaving and were deemed not critical during the first few months of the pandemic, when hospitals were focusing on treating COVID-19 patients and had concerns about spreading the virus to others. Secondly, patients were discouraged from coming to hospitals for other procedures, which also used our devices and disposable kits. However, as soon as the first patients recovered from COVID-19, their plasma was sought after, and plasma donations required an increased supply of some of our devices and disposable kits.

Convalescent plasma is an old treatment, typically deployed during epidemics caused by new pathogens, when other specific drugs or vaccines are not yet available. It is plasma (the liquid part of blood) obtained from patients who have recovered from the infection (convalesced) and have antibodies against the pathogen in their blood. These antibodies, transfused in plasma to newly infected patients, help them to fight the infection until they create enough of their own antibodies. This is called "passive immunity." It takes months or years to develop new drugs and vaccines, while convalescent plasma can be administered quickly as soon as there are recovered patients who can donate it. The downside is that convalescent plasma, always deployed under emergency circumstances, was never rigorously studied in randomized clinical trials. Since the beginning, there were both proponents and skeptics of this treatment.

Convalescent plasma was first mentioned in literature as a potential therapy during the 1918 Spanish influenza pandemic. More recently, it was used during the Ebola outbreak and outbreaks of other respiratory infections, including the 2009-2010 H1N1 influenza virus pandemic, the 2003 SARS-CoV-1 epidemic, and the 2012 MERS-CoV epidemic. Despite a low level of evidence and inconsistencies in available data, safety and efficacy results from animal studies, case series and cohort studies have triggered the widespread use of convalescent plasma for the treatment of COVID-19. In the United States, according to Secretary of Health and

Human Services Alex Azar Jr., more than 250,000 patients have been transfused, initially under the federally supported Expanded Access Program and later as a result of the Emergency Use Authorization (EUA). EUA has been mired in controversy due to exaggerated messages about convalescent plasma efficacy by members of the Trump administration and the perception that FDA was pressured to approve it. As a result, the treatment with convalescent plasma continues to be hotly debated.

So far, there is enough data on convalescent plasma to show safety, but efficacy has not been sufficiently proven through the gold standard, randomized and well-controlled clinical studies. A pandemic is an emergency and it is difficult to conduct well-controlled studies under such circumstances, for a variety of reasons. The implementation of randomized clinical studies is not always feasible, mostly because patients are potentially exposed to the harms of non-treatment when another effective treatment does not yet exist. In the case of COVID-19, patients' enrollment in such studies may be very challenging since many physicians believe that convalescent plasma can help to shorten the time to recovery and reduce mortality rates, as observed in previous pandemics. In addition, studies had different designs, methods and analyses, which led to inconsistent levels of evidence. Other major obstacles to conducting studies were the variations in pandemic levels and the difficulty to identify recovered donors owing to the high proportion of asymptomatic patients. Some studies ended prematurely because no more patients were available, as lockdowns resulted in few new cases of COVID-19. Despite these difficulties, thirty-nine studies with different levels of rigor are currently published and 155 studies are ongoing (as per October 2020 analysis of http://clinicaltrials.gov). The analysis of existing results indicates that convalescent plasma may be effective if given early to patients with COVID-19 and if it has high immune titers.

Our products play a vital role in providing convalescent plasma therapy, and we actively responded to this need by increasing the production of all related devices by 30%, on average. As part of the United Federation of Planets, we created a rapid task force to coordinate resource allocation across the organization, supporting changes in production, inventory management, scientific data generation, medical education, internal training, and customer support. To fulfill the demand, 150 additional associates were hired in our factory in Lakewood, and productivity was increased in the factory in Vietnam. The scientific team commissioned a study to prove that our pathogen reduction system inactivates the virus in blood products, and the medical affairs department reoriented its activities toward updating healthcare professionals on the emerging science of convalescent plasma and answering questions about available evidence for its therapeutic utilization. Sales associates were supporting customers who collected plasma on our devices. The focus on convalescent plasma helped to rally the company around our mission – *Contributing to Society Through Healthcare* – and instilled enthusiasm into the company, as we saw ourselves as one of the main contributors to fighting against COVID-19.

Most countries are experiencing the worst wave of COVID-19 yet. There is a long way to go until the pandemic gets under control, despite recent authorizations of Pfizer's and BioNTech's COVID-19 vaccines in a few countries and many other vaccines on the horizon. Lessons learned this year will serve us in early 2021 and after the pandemic. Successful companies and leaders will survive and thrive by becoming more resilient, through mindsets and process changes. My life has changed as well, and I doubt if I will ever come back to the previous ways of living and working.

I believe that even though science will get us out of this pandemic, art and creativity will help us to get through it. Creativity takes my mind off worries and ruminations when the artistic endeavors (still very amateurish) fully engage my brain. Fascinated with Japanese poetry, I started writing haiku during the pandemic (micro poetry, usually evoking images of nature and seasons) and combining it with nature photography. Writing haiku requires to concentrate on here and now, to capture nature in a mindful moment and turn it into a very short, minimalistic poem.

Successes and failures in addressing the virus indicate that the most successful approaches emerged from mindful leadership – empathetic, quieter, conversational, more caring, more socially responsible, transparent and not willing to risk lives. Overconfident, risk-taking, shooting-from-the hip, and broadcasting top-down leaders did not do so well during the pandemic and many put their countries and companies in danger. This lesson may change my leadership style and the type of leaders with whom I am willing to align myself.

Our ways of working have been challenged and now we know that productivity did not suffer when we stopped going to the office. Remote work suited me well, not only keeping me safer but also removing the stress of commuting and allowing me to spend more time in my happy place (the warm and sunny Nevada), near my favorite parks and canyons. As a result, my husband and I moved to Nevada permanently and I will continue teleworking from there after the pandemic.

But the biggest lesson from the pandemic is societal, not personal. Deep socio-economic inequalities resulted in significantly higher COVID-19 death rates in African Americans and Latinx communities in the US, especially in frontline workers who kept our sick taken care of and our communities running. The socio-economic determinants of health had been well known already, and yet as a society, we did very little to address them. The price we paid during the pandemic was very steep. How many more lives could we save if we only had a paid sick leave for all and universal health care? I hope that our collective guilt will push us to find solutions fast and that the post-pandemic society will become more equal.

A deep recession, worsened poverty, and increased inequality world-wide is on the horizon. We will not conquer the pandemic if we do not offer treatments and vaccines to all, and not just to citizens of developed countries. International non-governmental organizations, such as the Coalition for Epidemic Preparedness Innovations (CEPI), created mechanisms to distribute vaccines around the globe, to avoid vaccinating only developed nations and leaving everybody else behind. We should show solidarity and support this effort because the pandemic will not go away until 60%-70% of the worldwide population is immune to the virus, which can be only achieved through a global vaccination.

In summary, the pandemic has been a big lesson in humility. The virus is minuscule and yet brought us to our knees. Its only strategy is to infect as many people as possible and multiply. We cannot lower our guard now when there are still several months of the pandemic ahead. Science should continue to lead our decisions. We cannot allow the tiredness with masks and other anti-pandemic measures to weaken our vigilance, as long as the community spread is high.

The end of 2020 brought hope, as several COVID-19 vaccines are making their way through the development and the registration process. Three countries started to vaccinate their citizens by mid-December and many more will do so in the coming months. Despite challenges in vaccine manufacturing and distribution on a scale never experienced by humanity, I am certain that we will conquer all obstacles to get the world back on track.

2021 haiku:
the first star
on New Year's Eve
spark of hope

ABOUT THE AUTHOR

When Kasia was six years old, she had a minor surgery and was in a hospital for a few days. She was fascinated by medical equipment and what it could do for children's health. Back home, Kasia started treating her teddy bears with intravenous injections, which didn't end well for the teddy bears, but gave her a feeling of accomplishment. It did not come as a surprise that she became a doctor, several years later.

After joining the pharmaceutical industry, Kasia realized how big of an impact she could have on population health, through the introduction of novel treatments addressing major unmet needs, accompanied by medical education and proper access. She introduced several new medications and vaccines, and over the years saw their positive impact on morbidity and mortality.

Her chapter is about resilience in the face of the pandemic. She explains how she played a key role in leading her team — and the broader company of Terumo Blood and Cell Technologies — helping them to not just survive, but also thrive in 2020.

LinkedIn: www.linkedin.com/in/kasiaheinpeters
Twitter: www.twitter.com/Kasia_HP

14

MARC SNYDERMAN

FINDING MY WHY IN TURBULENT TIMES

THE EARLY YEARS

I'm a self-proclaimed disruptive entrepreneur. On the one hand, I made this proclamation to help set a goal to live up to a lofty title.

On the other hand, I believe that I've always been and only recently have been realizing that this is who I am. For clarity, I define disruptive not as trying to change entire markets, but rather as finding white space in a market to paint a new picture or draw a new process.

Case in point (yes, I'm a lawyer too): I started my first real business with my brother when I was 17 after almost a decade of working for my dad. We detailed cars for his used car dealership and provided a white glove pick-up and delivery service for customers where we went to their residence or business, picked up their cars, detailed them, and brought them back the same day. I still remember the business cards and flyers for Exoticare Auto Detailing we put on every car's windshield at the Cherry Hill Mall in Cherry Hill, NJ. It was a busy summer and a very profitable business.

A few years later, we tried our hands at entrepreneurship again when we were both in college and had no summer jobs lined up. We decided to open a hamburger and hot dog stand on the boardwalk in Seaside Heights

– yes, before Snooki and the crew, Seaside was a family town (just kidding it's always been the same). We knew NOTHING about the business but saw an opportunity and grabbed it. We called it the "99 Cent Eatery" and sold everything for 99 cents. It was a truly disruptive move – the boardwalk always priced high – it's a captive market and a short season – we realized our location wasn't favorable, and we needed to drive traffic. The other owners on the boardwalk were not happy with our pricing strategy, to say the least.

There's a whole lot to the story between 1993 and 2016, and you can't yada, yada, yada it, but I will anyway.

That's when I started my law firm with what I call #disruptivelawyering. We thrive on the concept that we're not like other firms and paint in the white space serving the small and mid-sized business market with pragmatic business and strategic advice on a subscription model basis. We take law back to its roots of being on the field during the game, not on the bench called in as a relief pitcher when the game may already be lost. I also decided to get involved with multiple tech start-ups and seed some other businesses of my own.

Before the pandemic, I was constantly on the move from meeting to meeting, trying to be seen as much as I could to build my network and find new clients and deals. I was traveling probably 3 weeks out of every month, back and forth between my office in Philadelphia and Southern New Jersey on the days I wasn't traveling. I'm so fortunate that one of my projects takes me to Montana frequently and I've really learned to thrive on the road. I enjoy hiking and taking photography and trying out food and wine and cocktails in every place I go (this will come back around). The same project that takes me to Montana had brought me across the globe to Japan and also, in the weeks before the US shutdown, to South Africa. It was an amazing experience that I'll never forget in one of the more dangerous cities I've ever been in, Johannesburg, but also met some of the most amazing people and saw gorgeous landscape and wildlife.

Travel was part of who I was pre-COVID. The late, great Anthony Bourdain once said:

"Travel changes you. As you move through this life and this world you change

things slightly, you leave marks behind, however small. And in return, life —
and travel — leaves marks on you."

I felt like travel defined me. The endless packing and running – the Instagram stories of where I was and the endless hustle. That was who I was, that's who I was known as – the guy on the move making deals and making it happen.

When I returned from South Africa, I had tickets to see Simon Sinek, the eternal optimist, in New York City. If you don't know Simon's work, he has one of the most watched Ted Talks in history on the Golden Circle of Why and helps us each find the true purpose in our lives. Simon says to find your why and talks about playing the infinite game in business, not looking for short-term wins and returns. There was talk of quarantine coming but I was not going to miss seeing my mentor speak in a small venue. Hearing him speak was inspiring, but little did I know at the time, it would become the foundation for helping me find my "why" during COVID.

THE PANDEMIC

As we all know the world drastically changed for all of us in the U.S. mid-March of 2020. I could no longer travel or go to my offices and networking events. In an instant I thought everything was going to be over. How could my businesses possibly survive this if it went on for more than a month or two? It's crazy and sad that my first instinct was really to think about business and not family – I'd like to think that it's because we had no idea how devastating the virus would be to human life, but in hindsight I don't believe my pre-COVID self would've thought any differently.

I decided if I had to stay home, I would start working out daily – trying to mix it up between running, yoga, cycling, and strength training. I have Irritable Bowel Syndrome (IBS) combined with a host of food allergies such as gluten and a fructose malabsorption and have struggled with debilitating depression. It's a bad recipe. This event had the makings of a catastrophic step backwards for me.

Depression is different for everyone. For me, it's like a giant dark hole that opens up and without falling somehow, you're just at the bottom – like being in a cave, all you do is seek out any bit of light to know that there's at least a way out. This didn't happen day 1 or even day 20 – it was around day 45 when I realized this wasn't ending anytime in the near future. I clearly remember sitting at my desk in my home office, looking out the window at a beautiful red robin and thinking this would be the next year or more of our lives. I spoke out loud and hung my head in my hands, "I can't do this." In an instant it was like a giant dark hole opened – in a hazy fog I went upstairs to my bedroom and climbed under the covers and hid as the darkness consumed me.

How will I get out of this?

I woke up the next day, drained and sad, but forced myself to jump on the treadmill then practice meditation about empathy. It's a word I had been using in social media postings and had heard so much from Gary Vee, but truth be told, I didn't really get. I made a commitment to myself at that time that for my family and my teams, I couldn't stay down in the hole; I had to find the light and knew that using kindness and empathy would help me find my way out.

The next day, I changed my entire routine and made sure I would shower and get dressed and "go to the office" downstairs in my house each day. I added in a standing desk and ordered proper technology and lighting for online meetings. These simple acts changed so much to build normalcy into work. I decided to push ahead and find opportunities in the pandemic, not accept all the reasons to fold up and hide. I spoke with some clients and colleagues and we decided to do an online wine tasting with Empathy Wines. They provided us their sommelier for a master class and we had great conversations on what empathy means. I started to assemble what a real strategy to lead through this pandemic looked like.

The answer was to pay it forward truly. If there was ever a time to step up and help others, this was it. Paying it forward creates light in the darkness, so I was committed to this path. I took a look at my portfolio of companies and my network to see what I could do. First, I decided to do a series of interview videos focused on small businesses that my firm represented to help tell their story and talk about handling the pandemic. While the videos didn't get the viewership I had hoped for, they met my goal –show that people are resilient and available for work.

I then saw an opportunity to ramp up my social postings across my companies and my own personal brand. I began sharing many articles, and my team worked hard to develop content that was tangible and usable for businesses of all sizes. We added a section to our site with COVID resources – from cybersecurity checklists and work-from-home policies to corporate communication samples. This social media blitz grew into developing a series of videos with legal tips. I said earlier that I saw Simon Sinek just before the quarantine lockdowns, and it really became a hallmark for how I have found my way through these times.

On a personal side, I have been home for over 7 months with no travel. This hasn't happened since before my children were born. In 2019 I think I traveled somewhere 35 weeks of the year, and when I don't travel, I'm in one of my offices and out of the house early and home in the early evening. So, there was a big adjustment for my family. I'm fortunate to have a home office, but I'm not the quietest person in the world, and I always take calls on speakerphone, and I'm not too fond of headsets, so my voice travels the house. We've tried to set boundaries in the house, and while my kids are in virtual school, we all retreat to our own sections of the house and stay out of each other's ways. There's been a huge upside to being home and spending more time as a real family unit. My daughter says she's listened to my networking pitch so many times she can do it by heart – so she finally knows what I do for a living! Bonus! My son is too busy playing Minecraft to notice.

My dog has absolutely loved having everyone home all the time, and there is no better way to work than with a pupster around to give you love and support. I very much miss getting dressed up daily, and I look forward to having a reason to put on nice clothes again, but when life and work are in the same place, it's ok to be a bit more comfortable.

One other bonus of being home so much has been having the time to cook. It's been an outlet for me to prepare and cook meals. I've always enjoyed it but only really cooked on weekends and now I can get in the kitchen during the week. I'm learning about middle eastern and specifically Israeli cuisine and really enjoying it. I bought Chef Michael Solomonov's cookbooks and watched a cooking show he did to understand flavor profiles and put dishes together. I started following the recipes but have branched out to create my own spin and am really enjoying this new world of flavors and foods.

But it's not been easy to stay positive and focused on paying it forward all the time. Some days the quarantine really beats you down.

When you're just sitting around and realize you can't see and hug your parents, when you want to have a drink at a bar with friends, or even just go to the office and hold meetings in person, the frustration level ramps up. We couldn't have imagined this would go on as long as it has. I got calls from so many companies that are struggling and trying to navigate the stimulus packages – I couldn't charge them for the time – it was my duty to help if I could.

The negative energy consumes you, and you need to find positivity. Like many of us do, I look for motivational quotes and try to find peace through meditation and exercise. I saw that Hewlett-Packard, Microsoft, Uber, Airbnb, to name a few, were born during recessions. So, I started to think about new concepts to launch besides pushing my core businesses forward.

I love cocktails and cocktail bars. One of the things I miss about travel is finding a great speakeasy in a new city and sitting at a bar and ordering interesting cocktails from the bartender. I've met some great people in my travels this way. My team has extraordinary capabilities in planning events. We looked back at the wine tasting event we did and thought – how can we marry these concepts? The Virtual Cocktail Club was born.

Launching businesses in COVID is not easy – supply chains are totally broken, and items sit on backorder for months – logistics and planning become critical skills along with leveraging existing relationships with vendors. Initial reactions to the business concept have been highly favorable and we look forward to expanding the concept significantly to help replace the cocktail bar networking that is lost in the quarantine world.

LESSONS LEARNED

Music is the backdrop to our lives. I was driving over to my office in September and Foo Fighters came on.

It's times like these you learn to live again
It's times like these you give and give again

It's times like these you learn to love again
It's times like these time and time again

If you don't know the song, it's rock'n'roll in a classic sense. The message is a clear path to deal with the pandemic. You need to accept and learn how to live. You need to give and love and accept our reality and move forward. That's really how I look back at the past 7 months and what I've learned.

I found my why.

I truly enjoy helping people. Small businesses need help growing and navigating the world. The winding career path I've been on has provided me so many great opportunities to learn across diverse business structures and concepts and I can pay it forward now. Practicing my why every day keeps me out of the darkness by bringing light to others.

I believe that many of the changes we've seen in the workplace and communications methods are not trends that will revert to pre-COVID when we are beyond the pandemic. I always try to lay out some pragmatic tips, so here goes.

Business Travel. The same day travel or 1-night trips for 1 meeting across the country are going to be a thing of the past. We have all figured out how to work on a video-conferencing platform – that technology will only continue to advance. The savings we've all seen from the travel reduction will outweigh the benefits of in person meetings. As someone that has been that road warrior leaving the house at 4 AM and returning home at 1:30AM for a day trip, this trend is one I'm looking forward to supporting. Those days were brutal!

So, get on board with video conferencing and don't be afraid to speak up that a meeting could be held virtually – but learn the tools and how to use them and buy a microphone and a light and fix your background!

Reduced Office Space. The need and usage of commercial office space will be forever changed. I have worked with remote teams for the past 2 decades and have known for a while that taking the office barriers down expands flexibility and talent pools so much. Large-scale offices with lots of open space are going to be a thing of the past. For companies that have embraced co-working and flexible space, there is little adoption needed, but others may have a more difficult time. I've been building my businesses on this model and it is fluid and adaptable.

145

Social Media Marketing. Digital marketing and social media are not going anywhere. They are the present and the future and will continue to evolve. You must participate on a company and individual basis. Your brand is more critical than ever before, and content is king. Don't sleep on building your profile and sharing content; you'll miss opportunities. Find your voice and use it; it's your chance to share your knowledge, the rewards are not just monetary.

Social Responsibility. It continues to become more and more important that your company demonstrate a commitment to social responsibility. Having a purpose, a "why" that is tied to ethical and social consciousness is expected and trends appear to be continuing along those lines.

The challenges of COVID are not behind us and we must remain vigilant. I'm hopeful that empathy and kindness can find their way back into our lexicon and practiced daily. I will do my part and continue to share and try to remain optimistic when things look darkest. I'll do my best to keep climbing the mountain and stay out of the dark holes. I implore you to dig deep in your heart and do the same.

Two simple words that have so much meaning are more critical than ever these days:

Be kind.

ABOUT THE AUTHOR

Marc Snyderman is the founder and CEO of Snyderman Law Group and the Co-Founder and COO of Apolline Group, LLC. He is a lawyer, disruptive entrepreneur, angel investor, educator, and speaker that looks to help small and mid-sized businesses grow and find opportunities to improve marketplaces.

Marc has significant experience as a General Counsel and Chief Operating Officer assisting companies with myriad legal and business issues. He specializes in government contracting, technology, engineering and software development, risk management, employment law, and strategic consulting as well as general corporate matters. Marc volunteers his time to serve on the Board of the Latin American Economic Development Association in Camden, New Jersey and supports various veterans' charities.

Marc received his Bachelor's degree cum laude in Political Science and Policy and Management Studies from Dickinson College, and his Juris Doctor degree from Rutgers University School of Law. He has his Executive Business Certificate from Notre Dame University's Mendoza School of Business.

Marc is married with two wonderful children and an amazing goldendoodle. He's an amateur chef and mixologist, loves good wine, and reads any management, culture, or leadership book he can get his hands on. He's an avid Peloton fitness junkie splitting time between running, spinning, strength training and yoga. His mantra is to "always #bekind and follow your why."

Website: *www.snydermanlawgroup.com*

MARISSA SNOW

THE COLLAPSE

In aviation, we are extensively trained for crisis scenarios. In many ways, we can mentally and physically go on autopilot, fueled by adrenaline and extensive planning for longer than the average Jane. The events of 2020 would test that training in ways we had never anticipated.

At the end of February, I booked a spontaneous ticket to Hawaii and gathered my small family to hop on a flight across the Pacific. Before COVID-19, the stress of the 24/7 communications gig was eating at me, and strangely, it felt like a 'last chance' escape. Little did I know at the time how spot-on my instincts would prove to be. We stayed at a beautiful resort in Honolulu at the Ko Olina beach, and savored long, slow days at the beach in perfect weather, and nighttime showings of *Frozen 2* on the lawn. That was the last week in February. Upon our return, the world had begun getting squeamish about COVID-19. Still, we thought we'd adapt and move on in a few weeks. It was an annoyance – a gnat, really, in the bigger plans for the year. I'd been through avian flu, then swine flu, in aviation. We'd figure it out.

But this time, of course, would be dramatically different. The fear became palpable. By March 10, we were altering procedures and game planning for a potential nationwide aviation ground-stop – a scenario that hadn't occurred since 9/11.

From there, the days became a blur. I felt my deep crisis training kick in as early-morning and late-night executive meetings were held. (While the East Coast and Pacific Northwest were experiencing spikes, Utah had yet to be significantly impacted, so we were still holding small group meetings in person). I remember one day looking around the table at the leadership team and recognizing the completely united front the group had formed behind a common purpose: to protect our people, our customers, and our business. Any organization has its politics, its posturing and ego plays, the cover-your-ass or siloed culture that can seep in. We certainly have had our share. But all of that seemed to evaporate as the group came together to strategize, troubleshoot, and execute. As a communicator, I'm always functioning best when the group is communicating, so of course, I appreciated the visible shift. However, I also heard others in the group comment on the shared camaraderie and effectiveness that went along with it.

We had many difficult decisions to make, especially in those early days. Working with counterparts across the industry – many of them the best in their fields – it was evident there wasn't a clear playbook for this situation. We were all feeling our way, fumbling through it, relying on each other and talking things through to get to the best answer, which changed frequently, especially in those early weeks. Transparency was the new currency if we were going to make it. Which made my job more demanding and rewarding than ever.

In many ways, I both observed and executed the daily tasks of procedural and policy changes, implementing them with warp speed across thousands of employees, trying to keep them informed as we adapted to the latest guidance and measure in place.

Doing the right thing is generally the most efficient thing. It also happens to be the safest. This lesson has manifested itself repeatedly during the past nine months.

SURVIVAL

I'm not a coffee drinker, but my stock of *Monster Zero Ultra* drinks was constantly depleted, and my team and I often worked through lunch and dinner to crank out the latest updates to all stakeholders. Sugar and caffeine were my sustenance – clearly a healthy diet during a pandemic. I may or may not have ordered a substantial supply of *Costco's* devilishly good *Kirkland* chocolate-covered almonds, which I kept at the ready on my desk. I went into 'survival mode.' While I was pushing through, I kept asking my team how they were doing, telling them to unplug and make sure they had an outlet, but I was still trying to power on. I kept thinking, I'll eat better/run more regularly again/get more sleep after we get through this COVID stuff. We all still thought it would last a few weeks, and certainly, once summer hit, the virus would be gone. We'd be heading back to normalcy by September. Haha.

The world gradually continued to shut down. My kids' spring break in mid-March was extended from one week to two – and then they never went back to school. My daughter would finish third grade online. My son's year of preschool never resumed. My colleagues and friends – and most of my employees – were sent to work from home. As part of the leadership team with a private workspace with a door, I continued to go into the office. I remember that pit in my stomach every day, desperate to work from home even a little bit so I could help my daughter with her school work. The guilt was enormous. We are fortunate to have a nanny, but we hired her to make sure my kids were fed and safe, not to help teach them, and she struggled with online school. One night, I came home to an assignment the nanny had helped with – and guided my daughter incorrectly through the whole project. I was exhausted – emotionally and mentally – and I had to help my girl re-do the entire assignment. I was livid. I lost it and almost fired the nanny that night. But the wave of anger that washed over me was enough to help me recognize there was more to this than that assignment. I recognized that the guilt I felt for not having been home to help in the first place fueled my rage. This was *my* job, and I wanted to be there. But I wasn't. And with unemployment leading news headlines every day, I felt guilty for feeling guilty – because I knew I was lucky to have a good job, particularly in my industry. My girl and I finished the assignment together – she knew exactly how to do it without being steered the wrong direction – and we got the kids to bed. I slogged to my bedroom, shut the door, sagged to the floor ,and cried.

I would fume for days, talking to my husband and friends about how my relationship with the nanny was not going to survive this pandemic. I researched Sylvan individual tutor prices and other backup options like neighborhood school pods, all of which seemed outlandish or impossible with my job.

It became clear this was not a short-term problem. The 'power through' mentality that had served so well in previous crises no longer applied. I needed a new strategy. I carved out time to set up a homeschool schedule and plan, and provided detailed instructions to my nanny and my daughter every morning, before leaving for work. My daughter and I went over assignments after my toddler went to bed, and prepared for the next day's lessons and assignments so we had a plan. We figured out the online school thing with very few mishaps for the rest of the year.

I religiously made sure I got a short run in a few times a week. I started drinking water again. To replace my coveted monthly massage (a social-distance no-no), I invested in a Theragun to help ease the newly permanent ache in my shoulders from sitting over a computer for far too many hours every day. And I made it a priority to mentally unplug each day and reminded my employees to do the same. My husband and I did everything we could to ensure home was our haven. Toddler snuggles and family bike rides became a daily ritual and respite. And it was in those moments I felt contentment – maybe for the first time in years.

We would spend nearly every weekend that summer at our cabin, 40 minutes away from our house but a world away and at least 20 degrees cooler (this is significant in the triple-digit Mojave desert) than home. We did puzzles and played board games. Our small family is closer than we've ever been, and fewer large family gatherings have made me appreciate my people more than ever. Dinnertime and bedtime stories and prayers have become heavily guarded rituals, and I'm so grateful my kids have each other.

It's been a year of trudging through the depths. Of digging deep and feeling as if I was scraping the bare bones – no meat, no soul, just bone. It's been a year of remembering the best of my colleagues and what makes teamwork truly special and transformative. A year of hard lessons repeated. Letting go. Giving in. And learning that I had so much more by doing so. Letting go of the misconception that as a woman, I had less to offer. That I knew less than everyone else did in the room. Because no matter which room you were in, nobody knew anything about how to deal with the massive challenge that swept in almost overnight and toppled everything like a stack of cards.

No leadership maxim gets you and your team through a pandemic. No training course prepares you for a virus that brings the world to a halt. For those of us in aviation, it felt like a literal interpretation of the sky falling.

As I write this, it's December and a new strain of COVID-19 has been discovered in the UK, sending a new wave of fear traveling around the globe. We don't know if a vaccine will be the panacea, or what the final toll may be. We don't know when we'll be able to enjoy a Hawaiian beach again or to go into a store without a mask. As we approach the Christmas holidays, the world feels fatigued under the pandemic's weight.

I don't have any brilliant nuggets of wisdom to share from these experiences. I don't have a new leadership mantra to light aspiring bright young minds. But here is what I've learned: we cannot survive without each other. We need connection and genuine shared humanity. Amid more technology and data than we have ever seen in our history, nothing is more powerful than the human connection. Every day, whether we want to admit it or not, we go about seeking it in one way or another. And I think we'll be better off if we embrace that fact, and together, find ways to propel forward, together.

ABOUT THE AUTHOR

Marissa Snow is the Head of Communications for SkyWest, Inc., overseeing public relations, brand, and internal communications for the world's largest regional airline company. She holds a fierce loyalty to her team and to authentic leadership and believes the best fulfillment comes from being a part of something greater than the self.

Marissa's chapter explores the experience of being in an industry that was among the first to feel the pandemic's impact, and the challenge of navigating the constantly moving horizon as the weeks turned into months.

Marissa studied journalism at Brigham Young University and has worked in airline communications for over 15 years. Leading various internal and external communications efforts at her company and across the regional airline industry, including web, marketing, and crisis communications, she and her team have received numerous awards for their work, including Platinum and Gold MarComm Awards for International Marketing and Communications Professionals.

She has been a competitive marathon runner and has qualified for the Boston Marathon several times. Now retired from the 26.2, Marissa finds herself running after her kids. She resides in beautiful St. George, Utah, with her husband, two children, and their cat.

LinkedIn: *www.linkedin.com/in/marissa-snow*

16

MICHELLE E. CLARK

2020 PERFECT VISION: LESSONS FROM A SANDWICH

2020 PERFECT VISION

It's 2020! "Perfect Vision, Perfect Year" Those are the exact words I was screaming at the top of my lungs while the mirror ball was falling.

The house was full of family and friends all around me for the 12th year in a row, hugging, laughing, and toasting the night away.

5...4...3...2...1... Happy New Year!

Well let's get real, it has not turned out to be so happy. In the flash of a couple of months, I woke up and I felt like my freedoms were on hold because of a respiratory illness caused by a virus called SARS-CoV-2, now commonly called COVID-19. I realized I took those freedoms for granted. Suddenly, I was working at home and after months, to my chagrin, this became the norm. I could no longer enjoy nights out, or in for that matter, with friends or family, and my daily trip to the gym was out, too. Well, maybe not daily, but you get my point.

Who would have thought that putting on a cloth or paper mask would become a fashion statement and a priority to stay alive? And who would have thought these two words, "social distancing" would require me to give up hugs and kisses as a special greeting to friends and family. Fast forward eight months and as I sit here on my deck sipping on a glass of wine, I no longer take these small freedoms for granted. I now cherish them.

PRE-PANDEMIC

Anyone who knows me knows I am a jetsetter, go-getter, and overachiever. Prior to the pandemic, I was traveling once or twice a month for events and family travel. Oftentimes, I would get text messages from my friends asking, "Are you in town or on a plane going somewhere?" Little did I know that on January 31, 2020, as I embarked on a plane to Miami (Yes — Superbowl Weekend) and on February 3 as I got off a plane from Oklahoma City, that would be the last time I set foot on a plane in 2020.

Never in my wildest dreams would I have thought I would be grounded for the rest of the year. Nooooo, not me. I had trips planned for Las Vegas, Orlando, San Francisco, Miami, Tampa, Dallas, Atlanta, U.S. Virgin Islands, the list goes on.

I had great plans for this year. This is was supposed to be a year of milestones to be celebrated face-to-face with family and friends with their choice of cuisine and location.

- February – my mom's 85th Birthday
- April – my in-laws' 60th Wedding Anniversary
- May – my son's 15th Birthday
- July – my father-in-law's 90th Birthday
- October – my husband's 50th Birthday and
- November – my toy poodle Lillie Rose's 2nd Birthday

Instead, we had to resort to Zoom parties and drive by food drop-offs or use UberEats to deliver the cuisine of choice at a designated time. I quickly became a grocery store order-taker on the weekend, a stay-at-home teacher and employee during the weekday, and party planner on the milestone days to make sure everyone stayed safe and happy during these times of uncertainty. Thank goodness we didn't live too far from one another or else it would have been even harder to bring smiles to everyone's faces.

As time went on, I was being pulled in so many directions and I still had to maintain and learn radical focus in both my professional and personal life. Work escalated and pivoted quickly to meet the needs of customers that were now relegated to their homes. I became a firefighter, very task-oriented, while at the same time I still had to plan for the future even in all this ambiguity. Family and work no longer had boundaries. I literally started feeling like a sandwich. Yes, a sandwich.

I heard about what people define as the sandwich generation. A generation where you are caring for a living parent or parents over the age of 65 and raising a child under the age of 18 while at the same time trying to maintain a career to support everyone emotionally and perhaps financially.

I AM FEELING LIKE A SANDWICH

As months passed me by it gave me time to reflect on how quickly life was passing me by. I quickly realized how much I was doing on fumes. I have a child under 18, a mother over 85, in-laws over 86, and a husband who just turned 50. I realized I was in the middle of working so hard to keep everything in play. Between managing the household, helping my child with homework, cooking meals for different families, and driving my mom to different doctors' offices, I was finding that I was spending little to no time taking care of myself. I no longer found time to go to the gym, call a friend, or even sit down and watch a movie with my family. Not in a bad way, it's just I am a nurturing and caring person by nature. I realized I was striving to reach the top of the professional ladder at the same time as keeping up with different generations' needs, without thinking twice about my own.

The lack of time for self-care caused me to notice a defined change in my mood and overall well-being. The responsibility of providing care for multiple individuals of varying ages weighed on my shoulders and I began to feel overwhelmed, over-stressed and under-appreciated.

So, what did I do? I planned a photo-shoot in July. Hair, nails, make-up artist, stylist, and photographer for four hours on a balmy Sunday afternoon. It was storming that morning and I was thinking: nothing is going to stop me now. My hair stylist came all the way from Atlanta just to put the right curl in the right place. Why? Because I needed to do something truly for me. I needed to be a little selfish for once in my life and do something I always dreamed of doing. I figured I am not getting any younger, so I might as well get some professional and playful pictures that really showed my personality during even a trying year. Yes, I was having a YOLO moment. The result was a clearer mind, a renewed sense of normalcy, an appreciation for me and the most important thing... a new LinkedIN profile picture.

By August, I was going stir crazy and really learning things about myself that I never knew. One of them was that I can binge watch many TV shows, and the other was the leadership style I possess worked well in the world we were now pivoting to. The COVID-19 pandemic opened doors to teleworking for most of the employees for the first time. I needed to allow telecommuting relationships to evolve naturally. We realized quickly that enforcing too many rules could stifle innovation, which I feel is fueled and enabled by trust. I had to suddenly stop looking at the challenges of COVID-19 and seek the opportunities it had revealed.

To quote Mahatma Gandhi: "In the midst of darkness, light persists."

LEADERSHIP LESSONS FROM A SANDWICH

As I mentioned before, family and work no longer had boundaries. My personal life transcended into my professional life. I quickly learned that patience, communication, and resilience were needed to maintain a sense of regularity. As time went on, and I quickly realized that things were not going to go back to the same, I had to figure out ways to keep connected with my colleagues as well as keep up the momentum that we had achieved prior to the pandemic.

As you can imagine, I am a very empathetic person and I want to make sure others are OK, even if I'm not. I wanted to make sure that the communication channels, the trust, and the fear were lessened with conversations, listening moments, and more check-ins. So, what lessons did I learn during this dark, tumultuous, uncertain time?

I learned to pivot like a basketball player and retained the teams' core strengths while giving the support to continue to think creatively by devising new ways to tackle the current situation. Part of the reason why I travelled so much is because I oversee and speak at the conferences and tradeshows my company attends. Along with my employees, who were used to also travelling, after about two months into the pandemic, everything was shifting to virtual. This can be disheartening when you are used to meeting with people face-to-face and implementing marketing plans with the core mission of engaging with people.

What was especially important to me was making sure everyone realized that they are not alone and that we were committed to working together to overcome obstacles. Moral support was key. Listening was key. Being accessible was key. And having fun was a must. An occasional meme would circulate to lighten the mood, a game night child friendly happy hour ensued, and a planned meeting to just talk about anything, but work became the norm. I wanted to keep people encouraged and positive even when I truly didn't have any answers about the future.

I will have to say that eight months in, I was proud to see the perseverance of my colleagues. Day in and day out, new directives were given, and the company pivoted and exceeded expectations. Regardless of the world we were living in, we must preserve and support others without convictions. In this time of crisis, I made sure the lines of communication were clear. As the old saying goes; there is no I in team and right now we needed to be the most unified, collaborative, and encouraging team possible. So, we encouraged brainstorming with colleagues in other divisions to identify ways to be more efficient, and created collaborative solutions as challenges arose.

COMMUNICATIONS LESSONS FROM A SANDWICH

Have you ever seen someone on a Zoom call for the umpteenth time and yet they still do not know how to turn on the camera? Then, ten other people just keep talking over one another and shouting out their solution without realizing what is going on behind the scenes? It doesn't help at all, right? It doesn't help at all because it's not a comprehension problem; it's a communication problem. If nothing else, the pandemic taught us patience and humility at the same time.

At this very moment, the use of all types of technology such as e-mail, smart devices (including a TV that I am using as my second monitor), videoconferences, social media, intranet, and some form of cloud-based file-sharing was heavily adopted in the blink of an eye. We all know that there are people in our workplace that are not as savvy as others when it comes to technology and we had to make everything work quickly.

Where? At home! I would bet that one of the top used words in 2020 is Telework. At the drop of a hat, many people were home — left to their own devices and internet speeds possibly shared with other family members, without a blueprint on how to communicate without being face-to-face. People had to quickly adjust their methods for communicating so collaboration can still happen, credibility can stay intact, and problem-solving can continue to produce new ideas.

Communication skills are incredibly important for a leader. As a leader, one of your jobs is to challenge the status quo and to solve problems. In order to achieve this, your teams should be mobilized and bought into the vision you have for the future of the company. During the pandemic, where changes were happening almost daily, the impact you had on people's livelihoods weighed heavily on the words and actions you displayed. In other words, you need credibility when the going gets tough.

I believe that leaders must constantly keep their head up and don't lose focus of these things because it is so easy to let the day-to-day tasks take over. You cannot do everything yourself. Just because someone is slacking, or they don't do it "your way" in times of crisis, you have to have trust and provide constant feedback to ensure success. It's not sustainable alone if you want to solve problems.

BEING A DAUGHTER LESSONS FROM A SANDWICH

I am a strong woman because a strong woman raised me, and I stand by that. However, it is so hard to see the vision of your mother you had as a child slip away. During the pandemic, it seems to me that the slipping was accelerated. She didn't want to leave the house. She no longer could go to her grandson's basketball games. We were scared to go see her more often for fear of unknowingly passing something to her. So, the routine food drop-off for the weekend was the norm for a little while. Then it became a long while. When you see people in short bursts, you don't realize the mental challenges they are trying to overcome, or the lack of movement causing the body to become weak. It is known that the pandemic is causing more and more people to be depressed. However, it is hard when a family member verbally says that.

So, what did I do? I went into super-daughter mode. After we took COVID tests, I convinced her to come over to the house to spend more quality time with the family. Three face masks on the face later, I made it happen. She seemed to get more energy just being in our presence. Then, as soon as doctors were allowing face-to-face appointments, we were there so he could tell her the same thing I was. But you know how some moms are—she would only believe the doctor. We started scheduling in-house physical training sessions so she can build up her strength and have someone else in her life to talk to about me (yes, I am an only child), and I started working one day a week at her house just to be close to her.

For good or bad, this is what COVID-19 has done to the circle of life. It has taken away the freedom and access to your elders and increased the fear and anxiety in our children.

PARENTING LESSONS FROM A SANDWICH

I must admit it has been very hard for my family to be relegated to our home with fear and uncertainty looming over our heads. As a parent, I could not show my fear, and I needed to make sure my son felt safe, kept some sort of a routine going, manage his hormonal shifts and emotions, as well as teach him ways to stay resilient and upbeat.

If you know anything about my son, he loves sports, especially basketball and football. Right before the pandemic, it was nothing for us to be out five days a week between basketball games and practices. During the time when all sports were off TV, it was as if the world came to an end. Even though he was 15, he still had all types of questions, mainly around what is this thing that is making him not see LeBron on TV. I quickly realized I had to educate myself so I can honestly relay the information to him. I had to read through the noise and discern what was appropriate to share, like basic hygiene practices, which anyone who has a 15-year-old boy knows does not necessarily come easy. In addition, when it got down to the face covering discussion, I had to search for sports teams. Thank goodness the Lakers won this year, a true highlight in his life, and I was able to find championship masks that he proudly wears.

I realized as time passed, many of the professional skills I honed were becoming implemented at home. My son became part of my team. I sometimes had to work my meetings around his schedule. We created a family schedule and workspaces that gave everyone freedom to do the best job they can under the circumstances. We rearranged a room for his classroom, and I became a part-time teacher. I became more involved in the PTSA and was designated the NAACP parent liaison to stay informed and influence the direction the school is taking on behalf of my son's education. I became the strategic partner to my son that I typically do with my colleagues. We collaborated more. We communicated more. We listened to each other more and we found ways to have fun. If there was ever a silver lining to 2020, it truly is the increased time I have been able to spend with my son.

BOTTOMLINE...BE THANKFUL

I have learned that we can't let life get in the way of living. We all have so much to be thankful for even in the midst of a pandemic. During a year where there's been so much loss of lives, where people have lost their jobs, where there's political and racial unrest and controversy, we still have so much to be thankful for. I believe...this too shall pass.

At this time, I keep hearing so many people say *I just want to forget 2020 and I can't wait until we get to 2021.* My hope is for everyone to pause and take a moment to think about what it is you're grateful for and how can you grow and learn from 2020. I am asking you to stop writing off 2020 and instead embrace everything that it has made us more aware of by looking inward at ourselves and outward to others.

If you woke up this morning and you're alive, be thankful. If you're breathing and healthy, be thankful. If you have friends you can check on, be thankful. If you have colleagues you can talk to, be thankful. If you can find something to laugh about daily, do it! I can go on and on, but essentially, we have so much to be grateful and thankful for so let's not write off this year. Instead let's run, hop, and jump into 2021.

5...4...3...2...1... Happy New Year!

Here we come 2021.

ABOUT THE AUTHOR

Michelle E. Clark is known as a #changeagent at Management Concepts, a provider of professional development, performance improvement, and human capital solutions for the government, where she is currently Director of Marketing and Strategic Partnerships. She is also the CEO of 707 Entertainment Group, LLC, a brand management and marketing consulting company.

Michelle is a forward-thinking executive with over 20 years of experience and prides herself as being an influential manager in the many capacities she is involved in. One of her employees has even told her, *"Michelle may be the most personally influential manager I've worked for. She leads with an obvious people-first mindset, and it was clear from day one that she was interested in helping her people succeed, find opportunities, and achieve, honestly, more than they thought they could."*

As a mid-career professional in the sandwich generation, she is constantly fighting the battle for work/life balance and has a unique perspective and approach on dealing with this on a day-to-day basis and in her chapter, she will explore how this has been adjusted during the pandemic.

Michelle holds a BA in Communications, Legal Institutions, Economics and Government and a MS in Justice, Law and Society from American University and is a certified PMP. She plays basketball and tennis, loves to travel and maintains a very heavy social schedule for her son, Justin.

Website: www.themichelleclark.com
LinkedIn: www.linkedin.com/in/michelleclark21

17

PAUL SMITH

A ROLLERCOASTER OF EMOTIONS

My name is Paul Smith. Yes, I know, it is a *very* common name. I am the founder of the Future Directors Institute, where I advocate and educate for the uncommon: inclusive, innovative, and truly diverse boardrooms.

It is strange to write your own story—who I am and what life was like pre-COVID-19. However, you'll need some context … so, here goes.

For the past five years – since establishing Future Directors – my mission has been to help boards and directors become more influential, more effective and ultimately, more impactful. It is my purpose. I believe creating a better world begins in the leadership we expect and witness from the people at the so-called 'top', and I truly love helping others realize that they can help shape a better future—from inside and outside of the boardroom.

We always start the year with big plans. I suspect, like me, you had some big plans for 2020, too.

My plans focused on two things: one professional, the other personal. I wanted to work on my mental and physical well-being, and I had plans to ramp up my mission through Future Directors.

As we have all learned, the universe is adept at throwing us curveballs that come hard and fast. The year 2020 was the ultimate curveball.

My family and I lived in New Zealand for a few years after moving from Australia, but we were restless. We entered 2020 with a discussion of *"where do we want to live?"* and had decided we wanted to make time for ourselves, attempt the digital nomad life, and take Future Directors into the virtual world. At the time, it was a risky move.

But where best to live, work and relax as digital nomads? Where could we focus on our minds and bodies? Where could we unwind from the non-stop nature of the world but still not hide away from it?

It had to be somewhere with sunshine and sandy beaches. Somewhere cheap but with great food. Somewhere far away but not too far.

Bali.

So, that was our plan.

My partner would take the year off to focus on herself and have a well-deserved break after ten years with the same organization. I would bring on more people to support the digital transition and have more time for my family and myself. No more travelling every few weeks. I had been averaging a hundred flights a year.

Little did I know that my wish would come true, though not in the way I had hoped.

My other plan centred on executing some big ideas. I have never had a problem with producing ideas. My problem is putting ideas into action. I wanted to stop 'thinking big, but acting small' and 2020 was to be the year I got big stuff done.

I was excited to bring more people in to help with this. As we quickly returned to Australia to prepare for our move to Bali, I prepared myself to mentally ease on the need to control everything in my business. Then, COVID-19 hit, and we lost control of it all, globally.

One of the words of the year was 'pivot.' Change comes naturally to me. In fact, it has since I was a child. Adapting to external change was easy. The ability to adapt to rapidly changing circumstances is a key aspect of leadership.

With the Bali plan scuppered before it began, we decided to plant our feet in sunny Brisbane until everything blew over. We were already living out of suitcases, and our new plan was to see out the next few months before getting back on track.

Yep. Another plan.

The universe had other ideas. Two weeks after moving to Brisbane, the entire country was locked down. Schools closed. Travel became non-existent. Toilet paper disappeared. You know the rest. We found ourselves trading beaches for balconies and sun for supermarkets. We were forced into the virtual world, whether we liked it or not.

However, as we watched COVID-19 make its way through the rest of the world, I actually felt happy – and grateful – being stuck where we were.

We thrived in lockdown. The lack of choice was actually a benefit. We ate well. We exercised daily. Work slowed. My creative partner became a creative teacher. I took my foot off the gas with work. Our options were limited, but this lack of choice encouraged us to maximise everything we were able to do.

I am still amazed at how productive we were in a time of lower productivity. On weekends, when choices would usually feel endless, the only things we could do is go for a walk, head to the shops for essentials, or just stay at home. But no matter what we did, our mindset was to make the most of it.

The world was on pause. Whatever you did, as long as you were surviving, you were okay.

Staying sane. Now, that is something different entirely.

If you are an entrepreneur or business owner, you can feel immense pressure to push, grow, and hustle. Constantly levelling up. Getting better. Always moving forward. It is worse when your purpose is to help create a better world and the world is crumbling around you. But with the COVID-19 pandemic, that pressure dissipated for me. It was wonderful. I could forgive my lack of forward momentum.

It felt as though I had one big scapegoat. The pandemic forced most of us into a hiatus from life, and I found myself thinking, "Finally, I've got something to blame if I fail." As any entrepreneur knows, the risk of failure is constant. Most businesses fail. Unexpectedly, the situation with COVID-19 minimised the intensity to which I felt that risk, because if anything failed, I could blame the pandemic.

It was as though I was delegating all responsibility to the pandemic, and quickly willing to place blame on it. To be honest, it felt good being able to feel like a victim, even just momentarily. I saw the attraction.

This is different from what I teach others and act in my board career. As a director, you are a steward. Many externalities impact what you can do, but ultimately, you're responsible – legally and morally. Governing is not just about turning up to board meetings. It is providing support. It is navigating risk. It is staying afloat. It is accountability in all directions. It is leadership.

I enjoyed the lack of pressure. I was able to focus on providing support to my community. But I was not practicing what I preached. I allowed myself to delegate my responsibility for my work to external circumstances, and not shouldering any, myself. I was letting my business go because it was easy to blame the effects of COVID-19, while taking on more responsibility for my community and my board duties.

This led to a lightbulb moment. Here we were, 'stuck' in lockdown in the middle of a global pandemic … in a great location, with just enough financial security to be able to take some time off work and focus on ourselves. Was I really stuck? Did I really have an excuse?

I realised I should not allow myself to postpone my plans. There was relaxing and taking time out for ourselves, but then there was coming to a complete halt. I decided to stop sitting back and letting life happen to me. I chose to adapt to the new normal, and continue to move forward.

So, we ramped up the production of our podcast and made some big pushes in securing new business partners. We converted our signature program (for aspiring board directors) into the world of Zoom. Most impressively to me, we quickly adapted our inaugural in-person governance summit, *Decision84*, to a virtual event. In addition, perhaps to my surprise, the switch to virtual made it more successful than I could have imagined.

We went from planning a boutique local event in Sydney for under a hundred people, with local speakers and attendees, to executing a virtual summit for hundreds, with local and overseas speakers and an international audience.

That was mid-June and after this, things started to get better. We took Future Directors' operations fully online and agreed to not go back. We found a certain level of acceleration with a fully digital presence, and we wanted to stick to it.

I realised I could not just sit back and be a victim of circumstances. I had to take responsibility, the same way I was coaching board directors to do. We were not shooting the lights out, but things were going well. I no longer felt like being a victim.

I made a plan for the rest of the year to launch new offerings.

Uh-oh.

Had I not learnt anything?

As my big ideas came back, I did what I inevitably do; I went back to my mission. The world. Change. Making a difference.

The Pandemic. Ugly politics. Climate change. Mental health. Division.

Even though things were going better for me, the next thing I experienced was a surge of emotion I did not expect.

Guilt.

There was so much suffering going on in the world, yet *we* were going okay. In fact, COVID-19 had helped.

When asked how I was, I felt guilty saying, "Great!" We were actually better off because of COVID-19. It took me a while to say that, and wow, it still feels difficult to write.

It was an emotional rollercoaster, and from this point of view, I often like to analogise life as an entrepreneur by likening it to Melbourne's weather!

Ok, this will only make sense to those that have lived or visited the Australian city. In Melbourne, you can experience **four seasons in one day**. It could be freezing in the morning, scorching hot by lunch, then windy and rainy by evening. The night could bring hailstones the size of golf balls. It is not every day, but it is often enough to be a thing.

As an entrepreneur, I say you often experience **four emotions in one day**. Like the seasons, these emotions can be vastly different, depending entirely on the prevailing winds. I was certainly experiencing the full range: anger, anxiety, joy, impatience, fear (for the world), and imposter syndrome. But that's what this pandemic has shown me. We all go through these feelings, every day. We just do not like to talk about, or even admit it to ourselves.

If 2020 has left us any better off, I hope it's in the space of mental health. We can now not only ask people more often if they are ok, but it's increasingly ok to answer honestly; rather than the obligatory "I'm fine" – which is code for "**F**ucked Up, **I**nsecure, **N**eurotic, and **E**motional."

I decided to explore this rollercoaster thing with others. The more I spoke to people, the more I realised there was a common theme. People had been experiencing these rapidly changing emotions, but not being able to grasp them or know who to talk to about them. This helped me realise my strengths as a facilitator, mentor, and coach. I was reaffirming my mission as a leader – not of a team of people, but a community of other leaders.

During the latter half of 2020, I learned just how essential our work was. My mission, both as a professional and a person, is to help create a better world. In my business, we do this by getting the right people, a diversity of backgrounds, voices and perspectives, into their ideal board-rooms. We help them cognitively perform at a high level.

They are the agents of change. I am just part of their support crew.

Working with my partners, coach, mentors and advisors (my community), I put this clearly articulated purpose to work. Being there for other people helped alleviate the guilt I felt. My mindset shifted, and I recognised that because I was doing ok, I could help others be ok too. Leading from myself helped me help other people, and I became comfortable communicating that more strongly than before.

The guilt disappeared as I realised that to be on purpose, I had to be ok. You cannot consistently help anyone if you are a mess.

Communicating this resonated with others. It turned out that many of us were going well but feeling bad about it. The more we talked about it, the more we supported each other to support others who were struggling.

After some time of not really feeling like myself, both before and during COVID-19, I was finally coming back to myself, feeling more comfortable in who I was. It was the reaffirmation I needed.

The more I was *in* service to myself, the more I could be *of* service to others.

Moreover, is that not what being a leader is all about? Being of service to others. It could be employees, customers, owners, the community, society and our shared environment. That is our job – to be in service to them all.

But reaffirming my greater purpose of being in service to others – with a focus on purpose-led boards and directors – led to another realisation.

I was exhausted.

I was doing ok and was available for others—and loved it—but I was getting up early to speak to one country, staying up late at night with another, 'meeting' with people virtually through different time zones. It had worn me down. It was like the jet-lag I had left behind, and I called it Zoom-lag.

Now, at this point, I must point out that we had shifted again as a family, across the country to Western Australia. It had taken us months to get here and I will not bore you with the reasons. For all my love of change, it turns out that change at the levels we were taking on is quite tiring.

The world was still despairing, people in my community were still despairing, and I was trying to provide support and hope wherever I could.

Hope is an interesting aspect of leadership.

Throughout 2020 and the pandemic, we witnessed different styles of leadership. There were the responses by those that decided to avoid responsibility and paint a picture of 'nothing to see here.' United States president, Donald Trump, who, after relentlessly denying the existence of COVID-19, took on the role of the victim or the president of Brazil, Jair Bolsonaro, who, when confronted with the number of deaths in his country earlier in the year, simply said: "So, what?" Then there were reactions from the likes of Jacinda Ardern, New Zealand's young female (coincidence?) prime minister, whose fast, firm, effective response to COVID-19 was applauded by her country and led to her being re-elected in an unprecedented landslide.

These vastly different responses to one common threat show us how imperative it is to have good leaders and to be good leaders. Prime Minister Ardern showed empathy, responsibility, vulnerability (to listen to experts) and strength through extremely turbulent times, especially when opponents in the media, business, and politics pushed for a different approach. She built trust and respect. She listened to a diverse range of voices, from scientists to business leaders, opposing politicians and the wider community. She consulted. She, and her party, may not have agreed, but they listened and learnt.

President Trump did nothing by comparison.

Whatever your politics—I am sure there will be some who do not like what I am writing—leadership *is* about character and integrity. It is about being in service to others and being responsible and accountable. It is about listening, learning, and supporting your people.

It is certainly not blaming others for your failings, calling your so-called enemies names, or firing (or disempowering) anyone who disagrees with you. That is bullying, not leadership.

As leaders, we know how important it is to be someone that people want to follow. Leaders need to encourage, empower and provide hope for the future. They need to be inclusive and seek to be the voice for those who cannot speak loudly enough.

With all the despairing things going on in the world, and after a brief pause, I tried to be that voice for my community. But it was a battle. Hope and despair. The emotional rollercoaster. Reading a bit of bad news, and waiting for the next, deepened the tiredness. I felt as though I was feeling not only my exhaustion but also my community's exhaustion, the world's exhaustion.

I believe society has experienced collective grief this year. Grief for how things were, grief in realising where we were going so wrong before COVID-19, grief for the things we couldn't change. Grief for what, and who, we had lost.

But I am also witnessing glimpses of hope. Hope that we will learn from this. Hope that such global trauma will create the mindset needed to change our future for the better. Hope that we can use this to see our individual and collective flaws, and hope that it will provide enough of us with the strength needed to change.

Hope is everything. We need it. I need it. However, to provide it, I have realized that I first need to be comfortable in my leadership.

Hope is empty without a plan. In addition, this year helped me to understand that purpose beats planning. My family and business both started with a Plan A, soon moved to Plan B, and ended up right through to what felt like Plan Z.

Very few people expected or planned for 2020 and the rapid adjustments we all had to make. Even if you expected a pandemic at some point, you could not have predicted what it led to, how it exposed us. But that's life. It is unpredictable. What we can do instead, is prepare for change, in advance.

I love a certain quote that is attributed to a Navy Seal. It goes something like this; "Under pressure, you don't rise to the occasion, you sink to the level of your training. That's why we train so hard."

I believe this is cannibalisation of another quote attributed to the ancient Greek poet Archilochus: "We don't rise to the level of our expectations; we fall to the level of our training."

Think about that as a leader. You train. You prepare. You get ready for the bad times so you can lead when others struggle.

One key aspect of doing this successfully is remembering that you are human and one of our inherent needs – whether you admit it or not – is other people. Even though this year we have all experienced loneliness on a grander scale than usual, remember no one who wants to be a great leader can be an island.

So, what have I learnt? Plans change. Shit happens. You adjust. You adapt as best as you can. You make the most of it. It might feel hard at first, and you can expect some cognitive pushback as the human brain is effective at focusing on negatives – but you can do it.

I cannot say 2021 will be brighter than 2020. Also, do not expect everything to become perfect when the clock hits midnight on December 31. An arbitrary date will not change anything; global pandemics do not abide by human calendars.

I can say that you can take steps towards helping to make a better 2021, and you can do it right now. Get on purpose. Discover or reaffirm your mission, your passion, and your values. Align your actions to these things. Do not get stuck waiting for something or someone to do it for you. Start building momentum now, while giving yourself ample time to rest.

Be in service to yourself and others.

But leaders, remember to forgive yourself any perceived failures you've experienced this year. We have all struggled—some more than others. That will not end, pandemic or not.

What we do next matters most.

We have all been stopped a little bit this year.

It is time to start again.

MINI-EPILOGUE

This chapter speaks of rollercoasters. You may have noted that I wrote this chapter to reflect this. It goes up, it goes down, and it goes in and out. Whatever you take away from reading my story, I hope you do not feel too sick.

ABOUT THE AUTHOR

Paul Smith has been described as one of the leading global thinkers on the future of boards and corporate governance. He has spoken around the world on the themes of generational diversity, director performance, and the future of the boardroom, from technology to inclusion. His business, Future Directors, is on a mission to transform the next generation of leaders into boardroom revolutionaries and in his chapter, we will learn what it's been like for directors to govern through a global pandemic.

Paul is an award-winning author with his first book *Right Seat Right Table: An Outsider's Guide to Securing the Ideal Board Role,* and serves on several boards including as Vice Chair of the Jane Goodall Institute Global, an international non-profit dedicated to expanding the legacy of iconic conservationalist and UN Messenger of Peace, Dr. Jane Goodall.

He is also a sought after mentor, board effectiveness coach, and podcast host — interviewing a who's who of young and experienced board directors from around the world. During the height of the pandemic, he also created one of the first virtual and international governance summits — Decision84 — which featured big conversations about the future, and the role of boards in shaping it.

LinkedIn: *www.linkedin.com/in/futurepaulsmith*
Website: *www.futuredirectors.com*
Podcast: *www.podcasts.apple.com/au/podcast/future-directors-podcast/id1317175077*
Book: *www.futuredirectors.com/book1*

RAM IYER

MY LEADERSHIP LESSONS FROM THE
PANDEMIC AND BAKING BREAD

#keepcalmandbakeon

"The pandemic is a portal." I love this metaphorical quote by one of my favorite authors, Arundhati Roy.

It is a gateway between one world and the next, where one can choose to be a pessimist and keep looking at all the negative or embrace the positive by being a learner and doing something anew. For me, it was baking bread.

One of the gifts of the pandemic was "time," the scarcest resource on the planet. Basically, you can buy anything, but you cannot buy time. The key for me was to tap into my passions to discover the best use of my time. As a family, one of the memories we cherished was the smell of freshly baked bread from the bakery for our Sunday breakfast, a tradition since my childhood. The aroma of a freshly baked loaf is a beautiful thing, really, one of the simple joys of my life. The sense of smell in humans is much more powerful than we think. It has the power to trigger strong emotions and reactions. While I was fortunate for the gift of time, the flipside was the misfortune of time taken away with friends and colleagues at work, which made me lonely. Given this solitary state of mind, my craving for the small joys in life was accentuated. This deep desire with a curiosity to learn got me started on my bread baking adventure. Baking bread is a surreal experience and, while I did satisfy my yearning and appetite, what was even sweeter was that it provided me the opportunity to reflect and learn. Here is a humble attempt by me to capture some of my leadership lessons:

1. IT IS OK TO FAIL

As an amateur baker, when I started, I experienced sunken bread, burnt crust, poor texture… all of which can be very disappointing at the end of the 3-plus hours of effort. It took all of 3 seconds for my excitement to turn to frustration when I witnessed the failure of my creation. This is a great life lesson: that things do not always go as planned, failure is as much a part of life as success is. Over the years, my approach to failure has evolved. If you have not failed, you have not tried hard enough to give it all that you have. To quote Friedrich Nietzsche, "That which does not kill us makes us stronger." We need to reimagine new ways of doing things in the pandemic, and we will fail as we experiment. It is important to interpret setbacks as momentary and changeable. The key here is to always operate with optimism and learn to diagnose what caused the failure and not repeat it. Learning to reflect on failure and keep improving is crucial; we all need to be resilient to emerge stronger post the pandemic.

2. DO NOT PROJECT PERFECTION, PROJECT FAILURE

I have taken as many pictures of lumpy bread, brick bread, burnt bread, salty bread, and a bread that had risen too much, as much as pretty, perfect ones. During the pandemic, like my #breadfails, there were moments of stress that led me to not listen enough. I have been passionate about my own ideas without listening to others and sometimes responded fast and furiously without thinking of the implications of my words and actions on others. It is important that as leaders we do not project perfection and be guarded at every step. As the French philosopher Descartes observed; perfect men are rare. Perhaps it is better said that perfect people are nowhere, and we are all imperfect at some point in time. We all need to model vulnerability and openly share and acknowledge our personal struggles, sloppy bread encounters, and silly mistakes including adding salt instead of sugar. So, as leaders you need to give yourself grace and, when your team members make a mistake, be gentle with candor. In my view, humility and vulnerability sparks more love and joy from others and most importantly builds even greater trust within our teams. As a leader, by modeling vulnerability, I have experienced a liberating feeling for myself, and my team feels safe to express ideas freely without the fear of being judged.

3. EXCELLENCE IS AN OUTCOME; PROCESS DISCIPLINE MATTERS

Baking is as much a science as an art. You need to follow the instructions, measures, steps, and process. I love a bread that has great texture, taste, and crust, but what is even better is to master a process that repeatedly delivers that perfect bread, which means doing it the right way by following the recipe. Today, we all live in a very competitive world driven by outcomes. I always love to win rather than lose, but we need to acknowledge that, as leaders, to deliver sustainable success you need to care about the process as much as, or even more than, the outcomes. Whilst following a process helps drive consistency of outcomes, doing it the right way with discipline drives sustainability. So, the next time when I say to my team, "I don't care how you get there, just get there," it calls for a moment for me to pause and think. It's important that I inspire my team with the values to take the right way to get there. There is a subtle difference between delivering and delivering excellence, as the latter demands process mastery and flawless execution with values.

4. EXCESS IN ANYTHING IS A DEFICIT

I love extra virgin olive oil and love the flavors of it to come through in my bread. However, one of the key reasons my bread used to fall was excess olive oil, so balance matters. Balance is key and one of the key reflections for me in the pandemic is that there is no such thing as work-life balance. It is all life; the balance must be within you. Keeping balance not just for you but members of your team as well is key for us, as leaders, to avoid our teams from falling. It is important to realize that if its only work and more work that you and your teams keep doing, you will never do great work. To achieve excellence, we need to make life a priority, we need to not only work, but live and reflect. Baking bread helped me do just that and bring back to my work a new perspective, which I perhaps would have never discovered. Especially during the pandemic, I have been a victim of #nonstop online meetings. I've lost precious opportunities for movement. Movement is key to finding balance in life as it makes us emotionally more stable and gives us the much-needed pause to decompress. Just like you can get the taste of olive oil in the bread, but you can't have too much of it as it causes the bread to fall, you may choose to take an extra dip of olive oil with the baked bread to enjoy the bite. In work too, you can have bursts of intensity, but to achieve excellence consistently and to avoid burn-out, you need to balance with movement and pause.

5. DO YOUR BEST AND LEAVE IT ALONE

One of the best lessons I learned while baking bread was that you have to follow all the steps of the preparation, but at some point, you have to leave it alone for it to rise well. As a leader, you need to provide clarity to your teams at the beginning, but teams rise only when you empower them and stop fussing over every step. One of the benefits of empowerment is that it has enabled me to create more strategic thinking time for myself, divorce myself from the nitty gritty, and provide clarity when teams struggle with ambiguity. In many ways it has been a win-win, as empowerment implies inspiring your teams with energy and having tremendous confidence and belief in your teams to execute and deliver success. However, one point of caution is that having confidence alone is not a substitute for clarity, to deliver excellence as leaders, one needs to provide the clarity. The resilience, grit, and flexibility my team demonstrated to adapt to the next normal once I had empowered them with clarity, always surprised me. It is kind of magical to see how empowerment transforms teams to deliver high-performance and impact even in challenging conditions.

6. PRESENTATION MATTERS

We need to keep in mind that bread may taste good, but great presentation adds value. Making it look good makes you feel good and motivates you to perform even better and raise the bar of excellence. I learned this from my manager, Gill Taylor, who sent this beautiful picture after I baked a pesto bread for her as a token of my gratitude for her leadership. She made my humble bread look so exquisite. Words do not always tell you the entire story, pictures do... as they transport your imaginary mind to new realms and evoke novel emotions.

Picture Credit: Gill Taylor

As a global leader of digital strategy and eCommerce, I have had the opportunity to work with complex Artificial Intelligence (AI) driven algorithms. However, one key reflection for me is that having a consumer centric UX (User Experience) flow and design matters more than a complex AI algorithm. It does not matter how brilliant the algorithm is unless the consumer can engage with it. A cleaner and more intuitive UX design can train AI and Machine Learning systems to learn better and get even smarter, but the opposite is not true. Great UX design is key to consumers engaging with technology, just like great presentation is key to stimulating emotions and satiating our taste buds to eat a great slice of bread.

7. PERSONALIZATION DEMANDS HIGH TOUCH MORE THAN HIGH TECH

Baking provides you an opportunity to personalize from thin crust to flour to nuts. When done right, a custom bread tastes much better than a standard option. However, personalization demands process mastery of the basic options, and focus on the brilliant basics. During the pandemic, the importance of personalization was heightened, as we were all in an era of constant distraction and need for instant gratification. We were often bombarded with messages and news that was not relevant and at times not even true as well. Customers are very fickle and in the Insta moments we live in, we often decide in a matter of seconds. If you can personalize and tailor your message to be relevant based on the behavior of individuals, just like a crusty pesto bread with toasted pine nuts which my son loves, you increase your odds to create brand love. Although we can leverage the power of technology, especially Artificial Intelligence (A.I.) and Machine Learning (M.L.) to personalize the content and experiences, the real challenge that I have seen as a digital leader is not as much with the technology as it is with the lack of human touch. We all crave the people skills, processes, and mindsets. Like while baking a custom bread, you need to think first about who is going to eat the bread and what they like. In marketing, too, it all starts with having a customer-first mindset. So, if you are not obsessed and in touch with your customers, no technology can help you achieve the full potential of personalization.

8. ORGANIZATION ENABLES AGILITY

Baking a great bread takes time. One thing I learned is that while you cannot reduce the overall bake time, getting organized with the right ingredients and ensuring a great prep is a game changer. Just like better organization enables agility in baking, as a leader I had the opportunity to reimagine my organization to drive better focus, clarity, and execution. To be honest, I was very nervous with the reorganization. However, when I focused on the "why" rather than the "what," it helped me to bring a fresh perspective for myself as well as my team. One of the key shifts was embedding some members of the digital team within the business teams to get them closer to the business and drive agility. Agility is a commonly used buzzword and often mistaken for speed in decision making. Reflecting on my baking experiences, you need to be fast in set-up but then stable and patient during the baking process itself. Personally, drawing from this the key insight for me is realizing that agility is all about creating an organization design that combines both speed and stability.

9. MINDSETS ARE ANTIDOTES TO DESPAIR

As a yogi I love to meditate every day. One ritual that has been extremely effective for me to start my day was what I learned from Dr. Michael Gervais, the sports psychologist for the Seattle Seahawks. He refers to it as the "Primer." Whilst I have been practicing this ritual for a few years, especially during the pandemic it has helped me to focus and prime my mind to create a mindset of being a "player" who can influence outcomes rather than being a "victim" of the external world that often forces us to think in a certain way. It boils down to three things; One Breath, One Gratitude and One Intention... all before you get out of bed every morning. Here is the daily Primer of 1-1-1:

- **One deep breath** – I avoid the temptation to jump off my bed and go for my smartphone to look at emails, text messages, calendar, and Instagram feed. Instead, I take a second, well actually 12 seconds, to ground myself in breathing. The key is to commit yourself to taking one deep breath followed by an exhale which you can feel throughout your body.
- **One thought of gratitude** – I then think of one thing for which I am really and truly grateful today; it could be my family, it could be my colleague, it could be a book, anything on the planet that makes me feel like the luckiest person on the planet. As in the deep breath, here the goal is getting fully immersed. So, for the days I baked, it is about the pleasure of enjoying a delicious loaf of bread or the smell of freshly baked bread or at times even gifting a loaf of freshly baked bread to one of my leaders or dear friends.
- **One intention for the day** - I then pick one thing I would like to accomplish for the day. It could be to write this chapter, getting on my Peloton ride, finishing an important task at work, helping someone get something done, or of course baking a great loaf of bread. The important thing is just making sure it is clear and you are able to complete your intention that day.

As Dr. Michael Gervais says, "Every day we have the opportunity to create a living masterpiece." This daily ritual helps me set my mind and baking my best bread by priming me into a mindset of excellence every day.

Finally, as a young man I grew up listening to ABBA: "Thank you for the music, the songs I'm singing." At this moment, as I am writing this chapter for this book, my first, I am truly grateful to be working for Microsoft, where living the growth mindset of reflection and learning is integral to our culture. As our CEO Satya Nadella inspires us, we need to be a "learn-all" vs. "know-all." As human beings we are all gifted and each one of us can tap into our passions to learn something new and create something magical; for me it was baking bread, for you it could be something else. The key is to kindle the spirit in you to #neverstoplearning.

ABOUT THE AUTHOR

"An eternal optimist and explorer who wants to leave the safe harbors of the known to blue oceans of the unknown to learn and achieve more" is Ram's personal philosophy. He is currently a Leadership Team Member of the Worldwide Consumer Channel Marketing organization, driving global Digital Strategy and eCommerce for Microsoft.

Ram has over two decades of diverse experience in digital, eCommerce, sales, marketing, and operations, two retail start-ups in skincare and fashion, telecom, and technology. His career has been one of constant and continuous learning. Ram loves to deal with ambiguity and is a hands-on leader with a winning attitude. His firm belief is that using the authority of "influence" works better than "power" in leading teams.

Ram has been recognized as one of the 50 Most Talented Retail Professionals by the CMO Council, Asia. He has also received Retailer of The Year Award by Economic Times for executing with Retail Excellence at Vodafone, India, and The Collective, a super-premium luxury retail store.

An avid reader of business books, he also loves to bike, a new passion since his move to the Pacific Northwest. A yogi who meditates daily, Ram is also a keen squash player. Happily married, he enjoys ballroom dancing with his wife on occasions, and playing cricket with his son during the summers.

LinkedIn: *www.linkedin.com/in/ramnarayaniyer*

19

RICK RICARDO

PURPOSE AND PROGRESS THROUGH THIS PANDEMIC

As I recall the end of 2019 and the start of the year 2020, my family and I had returned from our phenomenal nine-day, end-of-year vacation at the Campsites at Disney's Fort Wilderness Resort in Orlando, Florida!

Please take a moment to imagine with me our time there: spectacular holiday parades, the most beautiful, colorful, and creative fireworks imaginable, brightly lit and illuminated trees, Recreational Vehicles (RVs) decorated with hundreds of lights, and huge, glowing inflatable Disney characters. Hundreds of families and children, riding bikes, skateboarding, and enjoying "Santa's gifts," laughing and smiling. The Clydesdale horse-drawn carriage rides and the peaceful and serene evenings with the wildlife just coming alive all around us. The smell of hot chocolate and s'mores, grilled burgers, smoked ribs and steaks, and just memorable family time around our 26-foot RV travel trailer.

What a way to end 2019 and kick off 2020!

After a 30-year career in corporate America and now, as a business owner and consultant, one of my end-of-year practices has been to reflect on the prior year and ask:

- What have I learned?
- What must I stop doing?
- What must I start doing?
- What must I continue doing?

These questions have helped me evaluate my past experiences and then invest what I have learned in the future. I do not like living my life "out of a rearview mirror." I reflected, paused to clarify, and then charted the course to move forward. I made plans, created a strategy, and set goals for 2020 during one of those serene evenings under the stars at our campsite. I was ready and "pumped" for the upcoming big year!

Looking back, my family and I cherished those nine days now more than ever. Little did we know that our lives, our whole planet, would forever change just days after we returned from our fabulous vacation. On January 5th, The World Health Organization (W.H.O.) announced a mysterious coronavirus-related pneumonia in Wuhan, China, which we now know as COVID-19.

Who would have thought we would experience physical and social isolation, an increase in unemployment, a global recession, school and business lockdowns, heightened racial division, civil unrest, protests over injustice, and an election year unlike any other in history where our differences just exemplified how divided we really are?

My plans, strategy, and goals were not nearly as clear as to when I created them just several days past. My typical family and business life were rocked! Toilet paper, disinfectant, masks, and gloves were now the priority.

After the initial shock and realization that the pandemic was the real thing and that it was not going away any time soon, concern and worry crept in. Naturally, emotions were high. I remembered a line from the 1992 movie "Passenger 57" during a scene where a terrorist provoked the hero during an interrogation and was really "pushing the hero's buttons."

As the hero grabbed and slammed the terrorist up against the wall, the terrorist uttered a few words of wisdom that have, and continue, to help me face problems more effectively. The terrorist stated to the hero, *"Those are your emotions acting without the benefit of intellect."*

There was a considerable amount of emotions in my family and business. It was vital for me to filter through the news on social media and mainstream news outlets to deal with facts the best way possible. Leading through this pandemic with a rational calmness was critical. We needed to make sound decisions and not get "hyped up" by the media drama and craziness. Maintaining a healthy balance between my family time and business needs was extremely challenging. We needed to educate our emotions continuously.

I applied myself as I have done all of my life and in my career as an engineer and leader. What are the facts? What must I stop doing? What must I start doing? What must I continue doing? I accepted reality. Being a person of faith, I prayed the Serenity prayer, *"God, grant me the serenity to accept the things I cannot change, courage to change the things I can, and wisdom to know the difference."* God talked to me.

I decided circumstances do not determine where you can go; they determine where you start. I chose to be a victor and not a victim, to be a winner and not a whiner. Leadership is not an option, and my PURPOSE was more evident than ever.

"To make a difference with PEOPLE who want to make a difference, with VALUES that make a difference, with the ACTION needed to make a difference at a TIME when it makes a difference."

I re-evaluated my 2020 plans. I became more proficient with virtual meeting technology. Zoom became a household word. I belong to a men's Bible fellowship with a group of men that had I met through our local Christian academy where my daughter would graduate from in May 2020. We met on Friday mornings during the active school year terms. In 2020, I suggested that although we were physically distanced and could not meet in person, that we meet via Zoom. We did, and in 2020, we have never missed the Friday fellowship session. We turned adversity into an advantage. We added value to each other and supported each other as the Pastors, Providers, and Protectors of our homes. Quite honestly, had we not faced the COVID-19 pandemic and school lockdown, we would not have "stretched" our thinking and possibilities. Our fellowship group is now stronger than ever.

I am a member and leader in the Christian Business Men's Connection

(CBMC), a non-profit organization connecting business people in the marketplace. We held several monthly, in-person business luncheons in multiple cities and counties. We had to "raise our leadership lids" and innovate the means to continue to serve our community. We did not have the luxury to "go with the flow" and simply lock down and shut down. Our mission and calling were too great. We immediately "pivoted" our process and went virtual with our luncheons. We had more participation than ever, with business people attending from the cities and counties as well as from other states. We even started a CBMC Latino, and it continues to grow in service to others.

Why am I sharing this with you? The results we experienced by not letting the circumstances define our actions led to more service to others, more self-worth, more fellowship, and more hope.

- **Optimism** is the *belief* that things are going to get better.
- **Hope** is the *faith* that I can make things better.
- **Optimism** is a *passive* virtue.
- **Hope** is an *active* virtue.
- **Optimism** takes *no courage, no commitment.*
- **Hope** takes *a lot of courage and commitment.*

HOPE requires **HELP!**

Never has a quote resonated with me as the quote from Epictetus, *"It's not what happens to you, but how you react to it that matters."*[1]

One of my greatest blessings was to serve as a Ramsey Financial Master Coach in 2020. I served by helping and coaching people with their financial challenges during the second and third quarters of 2020. People were scared and hopeless. The average home in the United States cannot afford to pay for a $400 emergency without going into debt.[2] The student loan debt is over one trillion dollars. Again, now was not the time to ignore my community's real issues. I facilitated two nine-week classes to help individuals regain hope that this too would come to pass. They gained the knowledge and the hope that they could manage their finances through this pandemic. I helped them in creating a real and workable budget. It was not easy at times, but it was possible to win in their finances with hope fueled by desire and hard work. This resulted in the belief that they could make it and many happy faces. Hope was alive again for many people in my class. They will be stronger and ready for the next pandemic.

I was able to dedicate more time to self-growth and improvement. Why? Because you cannot give what you do not have.

The highlight of my 2020 year was the fact that my inner circle of people with values, integrity, and character increased. Jim Rohn said, *"You're The Average Of The Five People You Spend The Most Time With."* I have connected with many humble, servant leaders who have helped me lead with moral values and add value to me.

Leading through this pandemic has been a real honor. God has blessed me many times over.

Everything worthwhile in life is uphill; you cannot coast your way to the top of the mountain. Our greatest calling is to add value to others. 'We' is more important than 'me', 'who' is more important than 'how many.' What unites us is more significant than what divides us. What we focus on expands, focus on good values, good values expand, focus on differences, differences expand. For me, leading through this pandemic meant serving as a catalyst, a facilitator of hope that the best is yet to come.

As you read this book, reflect and discover your purpose; who were you designed to be? Many of us take this very often-used term for granted. It is also expressed as "finding your why,"[3] "what wakes you up in the morning?," or "your reason for living." The bottom line is if you do not discover who you were designed to be, you will wander aimlessly through life, complaining, and purposeless. When the next pandemic comes, will you be ready?

When you are at your best, being YOU... Ask yourself:

- What am I doing?
- Who am I with?
- Where am I?
- What am I feeling?
- In that moment, what is important to me?
- In that moment, what outcome am I seeking?

Next, cast a vision; what will it look like? The Bible states this quite simply in Proverbs 29:18, "Where there is no vision, the people perish."

- What legacy do you want to leave?
- What do you want to create? What is the outcome?
- What does it look like?
- What is the biggest/greatest picture you can see right now?
- What is the highest point you can see from where I am right now?
- How is your vision an expression of your Purpose?

Next, you must dig deep into your subconscious and destroy your B.S. (Bogus Story). Your Bogus Story is the reason you do not accomplish what you want to achieve. It is your excuses, the self-talk that holds you back.

Carl Jung stated, *"Until you make the unconscious conscious, it will direct your life, and you will call it 'FATE.'"*

- What story is holding you back from what you want?
- What story is getting in the way? What limiting self-image is getting in your way?
- What beliefs are out of alignment with your greater vision?
- What do you need to surrender to/let go of/lay to rest? (emotions, habits, beliefs)
- What are the consequences/costs/missing out on in life by not letting it go?
- What would be different if you did let it go?
- Write out the story you are LETTING GO of today!

Next, find your passion, your fuel. Passions make work play!

- What specifically do you love doing?
- What makes an activity special/significant to you?
- What do you receive from it?
- What makes a day more complete to you?

Finally, create a plan: strategically align your purpose and passion

- What is required? These are things that you have to do. If you do not do them, they don't get done.
- What gives you the greatest return? What gives you the greatest result for the least amount of effort?
- What gives you the greatest reward? What fulfills you the most: what fills you up, picks you up, and renews or recharges your batteries?
- What is your next step? What action do you need to take next? What are your first steps?
- Who do you need to be to execute? How do you need to show up?

My prayer for you all is that you become transformational leaders. That whatever you do is a result of who you are. That you are growth-minded and not goal-minded. We have to change for others to change. A transformational leader influences people to think, speak, and act to positively impact their lives and other people's lives. Become a sower, not a reaper. Focus on sowing seeds daily. Sow as many seeds as possible, sowing seeds without waiting for others; see a need, sow a seed.

Forgive and let go; everyone is human; see the good in people and help them. What you see is what you get; put a ten on the heads of the people you meet. Do you connect with or correct them? Connect.

When you value people, value is drawn from people. Be authentic. Continue to grow and evolve.

In August 2018, I gifted my daughter, Zoe, an opportunity to become a John Maxwell Team (JMT) member. She accepted, and we attended the live event at the Marriott's Orlando World Center—the largest Marriott in the world! She was amazed, overwhelmed, and complimented by all of the speakers and attendees she met. She heard comments such as, "*Wow, only 19, so young. You are an amazing young woman.*" And, "*Incredible. I wish my daughter would get certified.*" And, "*Your Dad must be very proud.*"

It was quite an experience for a young adult living in a social media-validation-crazed world where for most young adults, their self-worth is very questionable. A world where many young people find it impossible to think without simultaneously thinking about what other people would think about what they think. A world where eighty-one percent of people under thirty feel anxious, depressed, lonely, and hopeless at least once per week. And yes, I was a very proud dad. Little did I know the seed that had been planted in August 2018.

So fast-forward to Saturday, August 29th, 2020. I was pumped and ready to kick off my day by attending the first-ever, virtual International Maxwell Certification (IMC). I have been a John Maxwell Team (JMT) member and Executive Director since 2014, so I knew how transformational these events were, as I shared about Zoe. I received a text message from Zoe, which **was one of the most humbling and rewarding messages of my life!** Proverbs 22:6, *"Train up a child in the way he should go, And when he is old he will not depart from it."*

Unedited message from Zoe, 10:25am on August 29th, 2020;

"year 1: , year 2: , year 3: , papa, today is another year you have blessed and touched my life with value, 3 years with jmt but 21 years of my life. it maybe virtual & may be a different experience. BUT the value is equally the same. thank you so much for believing in me, touching my life everyday, believing in my abilities, and capabilities as a leader. both you and mom have believed in me always even when i don't believe in myself at times and i push and believe in myself because of you both. the blessings you both are in my life is unspeakable and i cry writing this all. brother, son, husband, mentor, Leader, christ follower, inspirational, certificated personal growth MASTER, engineer, friend, both captain america and superman in the flesh in his own way, are all titles you have had in your life but DAD is a title i get to say to loud and proud along with all those and more. i am so blessed to be your daughter, you have no idea. more than i express sometimes because it's something so emotional to me. i love you dearly and i am so proud of all you do to continue to grow. never stop. you serve as a role model that i only want to follow in and continue to grow to become. you have set the template of what i want in my future significant other because you are so good and admirable. mom is so lucky to have you, andie and i are blessed to have you. continue to add value to others as you always have because you touch lives, your reach has no limits. you fly like those eagles, but you soar beyond all limit and leave the most impact. i may not be waking up at 6:30 getting ready smelling your sometimes OVERLOAD OF COLOGNE LOL, being reminded of times to be in each room and huddle. but i woke up today with

excitement picturing you with me in that hotel except at a more luxurious place apt 5401 LOL i got my starbucks, pens, and notebook ready in front of me. i love you so much papa, let's get this virtual jmt dna, cheers to imc 2020."

Need I say any more? God has entrusted me with a blessed family: my beautiful wife, Vivian, of forty-one years and my miracle daughters, Andrea and Zoe, nineteen and twenty-one years of age, respectively. Be the leader to lead, not only through a pandemic. Lead people, family, friends, and colleagues through all aspects of their personal and business lives, lead your own life, and be a person of value and add value to others. Best of success and God bless you always.

---

1. References from John C. Maxwell (John Maxwell Team)
2. References from Ramsey Solutions
3. References from Melissa West (Blueprint for Success)

ABOUT THE AUTHOR

Roemer 'Rick' Ricardo is the President, Executive Coach, and Lead Consultant of RRR Consulting Services, a business execution and leadership company. Rick served over three decades in a professional career as an electrical engineer and leader in electrical utilities, including solar and wind energy generation, as well as engineering & information technology management at NextEra Energy, a Fortune 500 Company.

Since semi-retiring from his corporate career, Rick has continued his servant leadership by serving his clients and community as a personal and strategic business solutions provider. He helps individuals and small and large businesses/organizations/non-profits by equipping them with the skills to remove blocks and barriers that have stopped them from achieving their goals.

Rick moved to South Florida from Philadelphia, PA in 1968. He is married to Vivian, his wife for over forty years, and blessed with two daughters, Zoe and Andrea. Rick attends and serves at the Local Church in Davie, Florida. He is a student of self-improvement and leadership, adding value to others, enjoys the outdoors and camping in his RV, science fiction, movie trivia, and dedicating time to his family.

Website: *www.rrrconsultingservices.com*
LinkedIn: *www.linkedin.com/in/roemer-rick-ricardo-655226a2/*
Email: *rick@rrrconsultingservices.com*

SASHA STAIR

2020, A SOLAR ECLIPSE

From shadow to conscious leadership

Even before COVID-19, I felt the world was in a state of a corporate pandemic, calling for shift in how we lead in our professional and personal lives.

Ironically, our company was undergoing an organizational transformation just ahead of COVID-19 coming to life. Like all change, there also comes uncertainty that most of us are unprepared to hand. We don't exactly offer classes to teach people how to manage through, accept, and adapt to change. As a result, we—like many others—were already stumbling through the change like Bambi walking for the first time; determined but not quite graceful yet.

In a way, it was as if the universe knew something bigger was coming and organically, things began to shift. With our new leadership, a call for a different way of being and leading came. This new team was determined to shift our culture and they were making progress. Even still, there was a clear dichotomy building between paradigms of "old" and "new" leadership. For years, I have watched as leaders play politics, step on one another to get ahead, and care more about their personal agendas than doing what is right for the company, its people, and its clients. However, the call for a new paradigm is getting louder and slowly starting to drown out the "old" ways of leading.

Serendipitously, this "new way of being" is exactly how I have been all along. Transparent, authentic, vulnerable, and focused on being a servant leader. A leader who understands the importance of people and creating methods of engagement and connection to help people feel like they matter. My core authentic self was always this way, but the harsh reality of *corporate* took some lashes at my heart-centric leadership early on in my career. It took years of self-development work to regain confidence in my light. In time, I came to realize that no matter how hard others may try to dim your light, you cannot give in. The world needs more light and those who try to dim the light need us to shine the brightest.

Though 2020 started strong for our company, the turmoil in the world was continuing to unsettle more each day. COVID-19 and its impact was beyond what most of us could comprehend. As we shut down our office and moved to 100% virtual, I could feel the universe begging me and other leaders to shine our light brighter.

MY APPROACH TO LEADING THROUGH THE PANDEMIC

In every challenge, there is a gift, a lesson, and growth. COVID-19's gift to me was watching others around me begin to understand the *leadership language* I had been speaking my whole career. Leading through the pandemic for me became supporting others to see this new way of being and how they would have to adapt their way of leading and managing.

Leadership is not something you sum up in a few words. It takes on a different life and meaning to everyone. But for me, particularly through the pandemic, five key tenets stick out that have been critical for people to move through the challenges, get comfortable with virtual world, and to thrive in this new environment.

BE AUTHENTIC AND VULNERABLE

Authenticity is priceless and yet we give it away as if it were a commodity. We downplay our unique expressions because we are scared to be out on a limb by ourselves. We dim our light, scrunching ourselves into the round hole to be like others, only to realize this does nothing but damage our effectiveness as leaders and deprive our souls of true happiness.

I have often been told that I come across as "too nice" or "fake" until you get to know me. People at work worry that no one could possibly be this nice without an agenda. How depressing. I have been told, "you care too much" or "you need to not take things so personal." Well, guess what? News flash: I do care, I am nice, and I do take things personally because I am invested in my people, my clients, and my company. Are there things I can work on to stop some of these things from over-stressing me or pulling my focus? Of course, we all have areas to pay attention to and improve. But at my core these are personality traits that I cannot and will not discard. They are values that I live by because I believe in a better way of leading and being.

When I have team meetings and it has been a hard day, I tell my team it has been a hard day. Guess what? They are human too and they understand what a hard day looks and feels like. For everyone who has been taught that you have to "shield" your people from the harsh realities of life, that is a farce. If parents cannot fully shield children from the world, then don't bother trying to shield adults. They can handle it and by the way, they need to handle it. If they are ever going to sit in your seat and do your job, they need to know the pressures that come with the territory. That does not mean you do not still have sensitive information you either cannot share or have to time appropriately. However, it does mean that you can be more vulnerable in front of your people and trust that they will not see it as you being unfit to lead. Au contraire, vulnerability is leading. And we need it more than ever.

PEOPLE FIRST LEADERSHIP

I feel like a broken record most days because I never tire of saying, "people first." We did an exercise once at a company, where we had to score the importance of various initiatives to determine our priorities. I, along with a hand-full of other leaders, were asked to come together to score individually and collectively. I usually vote based on what is logical but that day, no one voted for people initiatives and I felt this overwhelming call in that moment, in that room, to be a representative for the people. I found myself sounding like a squeaky wheel but what the group ultimately realized was we were trying to combine two things that should not have been prioritized over one and other. One group of efforts was truly the investment work we would take on and the other group were things we really needed to invest in for our people separate from project work.

Without clients, you have no purpose, without a viable service or product to sell them, no revenue, and without people, you have no business. Our CEO says it almost every day; our people are our greatest asset and our secret sauce. We should all get this sentiment and focus our efforts as leaders to appreciate and provide care and feed for our people if we hope to have long-term success.

I remember, growing up, my parents stayed with their companies their entire careers. There was a sense of loyalty and family. As I entered the workforce and began to change jobs every few years, my parents were flabbergasted. The truth is, things have changed. Some of those changes are for the better given our current world. We had to evolve to meet the changing environments. But somewhere in those changes we lost our way with the importance of people. They became a line item on a budget to be cut when the goings get tough.

We lost sight of the people factor in more than just business, so many of us forget to love thy neighbor. To be willing to offer a helping hand when you can and graciously accept one when you need it. Our pride and egos have overtaken our ability to put others first and be servant leaders. We must find a way back to what matters and not take our people for granted. That does not mean we will not have to make hard decisions. It means that when we make hard decisions, it is for the right reasons and we hopefully learn to do better so we can avoid having to make those tough calls next time if possible.

DON'T JUST COMMUNICATE, ENGAGE

Engagement within your company and teams is the secret ingredient to your people's happiness in the workplace, which in turn creates productivity and a sense of belonging. With almost everything at work, I am a trial and error leader. I give something a shot. If it sticks, I hold. If it fails, I let go. During the pandemic, one of my favorite things that took hold was a weekly staff meeting with alternating topics.

As most months have four weeks, we focus our staff meetings each week on the following:

1. **Fireside Chats:** An open Q&A session so my team can ask me anything. I cannot always answer fully, but I always answer. And I think the team has appreciated the transparency and feeling that they are worthy of the time and effort to listen and provide as much information as I can. It seems so simple, yet it is a common missed opportunity to connect with our people by just being present and engaged.

2. **Kanban Highlights:** Department leads provide highlights of work in progress, accomplishments, and challenges. When we were physically in the office, we had a Kanban board we reviewed each week. We tried a virtual Kanban using various tools and it just didn't fit for us. So, we moved to once a month leads from each department providing key updates. That way the teams have a chance to present work in progress and keep the full team informed. The smaller teams then used their daily scrums to work through the tactical in progress, backlog, and blockers.

3. **Show & Tell:** A person from our team chooses a personal or professional topic as an opportunity to teach the rest of the team something new. Two of my favorites were learning about professional cycling and the essentials of buying your bike, as well as the culture and history of Nigeria, a team member's home country.

4. **Guest Speaker:** I invite a lead from another division to come share with my team about what their function is and how it fits in at our company. This gave an opportunity for my team to learn more about what we do in other areas within our company and for the guest to get to know my team.

After trying on a few models for our staff meetings, this one was the winner. I love doing surveys with my team as we try things on. The response to this model was the most positive so we stuck with it and that resulted in increased connection and engagement within our team and with others in the organization.

Another point of engagement I created, which arguably is the most important thing I do, is called *Monday Magic*. What started as a "Monday Memo" to my team over a year later has now become a point of inspiration for most of our company. The concept was simple: engage and connect at an authentic level with my team. I put myself in their shoes. If I were managing through the change, a bit of inspiration and transparent communication to keep me informed and engaged would help bring comfort. So, that is what I did. Each memo included a quote and a personal story relative to how the words in the quote had impacted or played out in my life. It then included "things going on" at our company for the week, and "shout outs" to acknowledge people and teams for their hard work. The distribution list kept growing and the initial response was so positive that I thought, "Hey, I may be on to something here."

I have since renamed the memo, *Monday Magic*, with a focus on inspiration. The distribution list has grown and is now posted on our Women's Resource Group teams page too, as well as on my LinkedIn feed.

CREATE A SAFE SPACE TO BE REAL

I am not sure when the joke of "Hollywood fake" became the norm, but I would really like us to let that one go. In my career, I have watched so many leaders either fake it, or put on a façade, or feel the need to be superman/woman and never show any fault. None of which works.

Especially now more than ever, the reality of life is upon us. People are working from home while raising their kids. Our normal check in with our managers has now been spiced up with finger painting with kindergarteners, or an arithmetic question from our fifth grader or my personal favorite, the college student home for the week that has high demands of our attention. Whatever the flavor, it is near impossible to shield your personal life from work in this odd pandemic environment.

Instead of trying to hide from it or fight it, our company has embraced it. Not only providing flexibility with remote work, schedule, and time off but in accepting the kid being on your lap or the dog barking in the background. It is the way life is now and there is no point trying to hide from it. The more real we are with one and other, the more we bond, have compassion, and learn to chill out.

Taking it a step further, I really tune into my team. If we get onto a call and I can tell the tension is high, or people are tired, I call it like I see it. Especially if it is me! I will say things like, "No one is at their best 100% of the time. It is okay to have a day where you are not as productive and need to take a break and go for a walk. Some days are just not our best days, and it is okay. We are human." Alternatively, I will ask everyone to take a few deep breaths and just let go of what is swirling around in their minds to help ground people in the current meeting.

Especially in this remote environment, we click from one meeting to the next without breaks – mental, physical, biological…we must take breaks. It is ridiculous to think people can function without going insane with no breaks. Acknowledge we need space to adjust to this crazy new way of being and permission to be real through it all.

WHAT IT MEANS TO BE "IN IT TOGETHER"

Now more than ever, we are in this together. We all have circumstances that are impacting our ability to work the way we used to. Whether family in the home, people battling illness, or the gardener blowing leaves at your window, the days of having an office work environment are mostly gone. Moreover, it is not as if we were given a heads up or a manual to prepare for this change. It just hit like a brick wall and we all had to adjust fast while dealing with the uncertainty and fear of a new virus.

In these times of uncertainty, we should turn *to* one and another to get through. I have watched as people at our company have mailed care packages or dropped off food to others recovering from COVID-19. I have relished reading about people's staycations on our company teams page and been impressed in all the creative ways our company brings us together whether through music, stories, or virtual scavenger hunts for families. It is surprising how much we can still do in a remote environment to connect, engage, and find a new way of being in this pandemic together.

Just like anything new, it takes some time to adapt to the changes. Try on new things for size, go back to the drawing board and adjust then try again. The key for me through it all has been focusing on the people and shining my light. I have seen firsthand how the right focus and intention with a lot of persistence and patience can help us shift like an eclipse from shadow to conscious leadership.

ABOUT THE AUTHOR

Sasha Stair, known as the *spiritual warrior leader*, has a passion for helping people and companies grow through conscious and transformational leadership. With significant experience facilitating business transformation—from conception to execution—she brings emotionally intelligent leadership across people, process, and technology to deliver results, and drive innovation.

Known as a risk-taker, Sasha has often chosen roles in her career that require self-transformation and reinvention. Consequently, she offers a unique skill set, spanning relationship cultivation and management, service delivery, strategy, sales, business growth, consulting, IT, and business operations with experience across multiple industries.

As an emotionally intelligent leader, her transparent and open communication style has provided a critical framework for cultivating trust, teamwork and collaboration, and has been an essential component of program performance.

Sasha is currently an executive in the financial services industry, transitioning from leading and running IT business operations to a new role in her firm to create and lead client delivery across new business, products, and services. She resides in Scottsdale, Arizona with her husband, Matt, and their daughter is currently a pre-med student at Northern Arizona University in Flagstaff.

LinkedIn: *www.linkedin.com/in/sashastair*

21

SUZANNE O'BRIEN

GREAT EXPECTATIONS; NEW REALITY

I thought about starting my own company for at least the five years prior to that, but was always too afraid. Then something happened that pushed me to finally take a chance on myself.

I was seven months pregnant and my son was a year and a half. It was a shock when I found out that I was pregnant with my second child. I had four miscarriages before that, the last two being at ten and twelve weeks, respectively. She would be our rainbow baby, and we were so excited! I honestly think that this is the first time that I have shared that outside of my thoughts. I am a strong person who can handle anything, but the feeling that your body has betrayed you or somehow you are not meant to carry your baby is something you cannot get out of your head or even forgive yourself for, although it isn't even something you can control.

So there I was one night in my living room. My husband, Jeff, and son, Jax, were asleep, and I founded Blake Rian Consulting, which I named after my soon-to-be born daughter. I didn't have the option to fail. I built my business with the vision to build meaningful, long-lasting relationships with all of our clients and candidates. The goal would be to become the clients' business partner throughout the hiring process. Our success would be a result of our commitment to the best people, the best solutions, and the best results. I had seen over the last few years and the few 'corporate' roles that I had been in that relationships were not the focus. The bottom-line profit was the focus. I saw companies underpay contractors so they could make a higher gross margin, bill clients at a 100% markup (who probably had no idea it was happening), and turn away business — I mean huge potential accounts — because it didn't have a high enough markup. For the first time I realized 'staffing' had become a bad word. That was not how I wanted it to be. It is not how I want to do business, and enough was enough. It was time to get back to what 'staffing' was when I got into this industry — building long term partnerships/relationships and doing what is best for the client and the candidate!

The first question I would get is, "What do you specialize in?" I am a firm believer that you don't specialize in something unless you have done the job. You will see many agencies that say they are the subject matter expert in something, when really they have taken someone outside of that industry and trained them for 30-60 days, if that, on how to sell themselves as the SME. You will find that agencies also use that as a way to win and turn away business. I didn't want to limit myself to industries or "specialties" that I staffed for. I didn't want the client to feel that they needed to fit into our business model. I wanted to fit into theirs! I decided we would work on all verticals and our partnership would include Contract, Direct Hire, Payroll Services and Managed Services opportunities. Blake Rian Consulting would provide an efficient, effective, and enjoyable experience to job seekers and employers in all industries nationwide. I found myself reiterating what I have said my whole career; I know that a resume is important, but it is just a blueprint of someone's experience. Our job is to understand the needs of the employers and job seekers to help bring together the perfect match in expertise, skill, and company culture fit. We are committed to providing you, our clients, with an experience focused on what you value most.

The first two months, I didn't sleep very well as the thoughts of how I was going to do this kept running through my head. Am I making the right decision? What I found was that the clients I kept relationships with for the previous five to six years were the first ones to sign my contracts. I realized that what I thought all along about relationships being the foundation of our business really was! My first year was fun and exciting as I exceeded my expectations and the revenue goals I had set for myself. I was setting up my plans and goals for 2020, and I was so pumped to exceed the prior year and continue to grow!

Little did I know the universe had other plans.

I remember hearing about COVID-19 as early as January and thinking it was just like when the big scare around shingles happened. Everyone was so worried, and you would hear about it all over the news. I remember my son having an allergic reaction to an antibiotic and getting a rash. I was convinced that is what it was and rushed him to Seattle Children's ER. It wasn't shingles, though, and he was fine. Suddenly shingles blew over and no one was talking about it anymore. Later, we would hear about Ebola and how scary that it was. And then we were told to worry about Zika virus; but these huge news stories seemed to go away in a month or two. That is what I thought COVID-19 would do, but boy was I wrong. Once we heard it was in Kirkland, WA where we lived, we decided to pull our son out of school on February 7th. Our son has Reactive Airway Disease as a result of being born a month early. Any time he gets a cold, he is in the ER on a nebulizer, and one very scary time we had to ride in an ambulance. We decided better to be safe than sorry.

As this was going on, I was still expecting it to be done in a couple of months. I moved forward and planned what 2020 was going to look like. Then March hit and everything turned upside down. I had clients who were unsure of what the next month was going to bring and what their business needs would be. Then the world shut down. Naively, I still thought OK, we can do this and hunker down for a month or so and everything will go back to normal. And then it didn't....

In the midst of all of this, we were trying to decide if we were going to move. Our son's breathing was getting worse each time he got sick and it was becoming more frequent. After speaking to his pediatricians and specialists, they recommended a drier climate for him. We then made the tough decision to move to California. We had been visiting Newport Beach and loved the area, but all of our immediate family was in WA. Then came the questions around our plans to move; would the states be shut down? Luckily, we were able to pack up and go.

Moving through the pandemic was very scary and sad. Due to COVID-19, we were not able to say goodbye to everyone we wanted to, family included. During all of this, I was still trying to figure out what was going on with my clients and, essentially, my business. Then April hit and everything came crashing down. My largest client stopped operations, and my other clients froze all hiring plans. I built the majority of my budget around my largest client with the flexibility to grow my business. Why did I do this? I don't know!

I know better in this industry that you never build your business around one client. Diversifying your portfolio is a *must*. I've even trained employees on this! Genuinely, the reason you should not do this is if this client goes away, so does your business. At this point, panic started setting in and I asked myself how I was going to do this. How would I keep my business going and my employees employed and feed my family? It is so different when everything rides on you and there is no one else sending you a paycheck. I felt the weight of my employees' lives on my shoulders as well. I didn't want to disappoint them or even worse, let them go. It was interesting as a business owner to have the inner struggle of who do I save first? Myself and family or my team? My team had put so much time and work into what I was building, and the last thing I wanted them to feel was 'expendable.'

When I started my business, I used my own funds and did not have any investors or business loans. For the first six months, it was just me doing everything. Then I started transitioning our nanny, Corrissa, into the business. She saved our lives by keeping me organized and watching Blake. She has moved from Nanny to Operations Specialist and now to my Operations Supervisor. She is my right hand, and I am not kidding when I say I would be lost without her! As the business slowed, the funds thinned. The month of May hit and the fear started to set in again: am I going to make it? Was this all for nothing? How am I going to make payroll? What if I can't buy groceries for my own family, and again, what about my team? It was in that moment I had to dig deep inside myself and say, "Look this is going to work. You will figure something out and won't fail. You can't fail."

Keeping in mind that during all of this we were in lockdown in our house with a one-year-old, three-year-old, two Rottweilers and a cat. Our house was crazy, and our three-year-old son was starting to feel the isolation from not having friends and not going to school. He was supposed to go to this amazing summer camp, which of course was cancelled. As an adult, it is hard sometimes to stop and think about how little kids are affected. You just think, "Oh, they love hanging out with mom and dad, they won't notice," but that is not true. He would see kids and say, "I want to go play with my friends." Then the mom guilt comes on and you know even though you are doing what you have to in order to keep them safe, you also want them to have fun and be happy.

As if that craziness were not enough, I had a difficult time healing from Blake's C-Section. I have constant pain along the right side of my suture line. I ended up with a very bad case of Diastasis Recti, which is when your muscles never go back together. Although Blake is almost two years old, I still look like I am nine months pregnant. It is extremely frustrating and very physically tough, as I have zero core muscles. I struggle with back strain constantly because I have no abdominal muscles, and I cannot exercise or do very strenuous activity due to the pain. The only fix is surgery and interestingly enough, health insurance only covers it for men. I literally have thousands of things I am thinking about throughout the day as far as everyday life and how to make this work.

Even with that on my mind, I kept pushing forward and reaching out to new industries and companies trying to drum up business. I had it in my mind that no matter what happened next, I would find a way to pivot. I had worked too hard throughout my career to stop now. I was so happy to find out a PPP was coming, and I was ready to submit my information. I went to my bank, where I have all of my personal and business accounts and credit cards. I never heard back from them. I was shocked and worried now. Luckily, a friend of mine referred me to her boutique bank in New York, and they were able to help me apply at the wire. Those funds were a blessing, and I was able to rest a little easier knowing that my employees would be ok for the next few weeks at least.

I shifted my focus again to pushing sales and trying to build new relationships with clients. I went back to the basics: ad calls. I remember early in my career doing these and training my teams on how to make them. It had been a while I must say, but still just as fun. I spoke to a woman named Sara at The Sophia Way, who was looking for an AP person. They had been struggling to find someone and had been looking for months. She let me know that they are a non-profit and could not afford to pay an agency to help them hire. I thanked her for the conversation and let her know I enjoyed chatting with her. We hung up. I sat there for a minute and thought about all of the struggles I had been through the last few months and the way I could have benefited from a bank or lender helping me. I called her back and said, "I really want to help you, because I believe in what your organization does, and it is the right thing to do." We found her a great candidate at no cost to them. I believe that what you put out in the world comes back to you. I think now of all times we have had to be kind and help each other get through this pandemic. I also believe that long-term relationships and partnerships are what is most important in this industry and the world.

We were also happy to be able to support another cause in Southern California, CASA. The organization helps children in the Orange County area who are in the foster care system by giving them appointed advocates to help them during their time in the court system and foster care.

So there we were in June and the news was still bleak, as far as the virus goes, and we were shutting down again. I had to think carefully about what I could do to keep things moving. I shifted my industry and started looking at healthcare. It is an industry more in-demand than ever! It is not going anywhere; however, it is super-competitive. I knew I had to do something, so I went for it! We opened a Health Care division focusing on clinical and non-clinical positions. We have been lucky to partner with a company as a sub-vendor and have a plethora of open roles to recruit on. I was excited to jump in and tackle this industry, as I had managed health-care recruiting teams before.

I also had the pleasant surprise of one of my best friends wanting to work with me! She was new to the industry but super outgoing and I knew she would be a great fit! She came onboard just as I was breaking into a few new clients in the title & escrow industry. She was able to close business and find amazing candidates for our clients extremely fast due to her hard work and dedication. I felt things were looking up and we were going to be OK. By August we had a groove of things moving in the right direction, and I felt more relaxed. Maybe things are going to get much better and we will see some normalcy, I thought. We found out Jax could attend in-person school in September, so we were excited for him and he was over the moon! All of this going on reminded me that staying positive and putting good things in the universe will come back to you!

We have been extremely fortunate that the coronavirus has not directly affected our family. We are also very diligent with social distancing and staying home. Jax is loving school and we love that he can enjoy that again. I think that is the most important thing: to be cautious and aware of things around you.

I HAVE to say after going through everything in 2020 and still facing so much uncertainty ahead, I have to look at the positive. I have to remind myself that I am still very fortunate and that so many other people, businesses, and families have suffered much more tragedy. I feel like my main takeaways this year as a business owner are to always push forward, never stop trying, and *never* stop believing in yourself. As a woman, I have learned that I really can do anything I put my mind to. I can run my business, raise my beautiful children, and have a successful relationship with my other half. As a mother, part of me is thankful for the shut down in the sense I had more time to spend with my children. I was able to spend invaluable time with them that I will never get back! They also get to see Mommy working and I have seen pride in their eyes.

I truly hope that everyone who is struggling, whether, in business, finances, health or in any other manner keep their head up and look toward the future. I am very determined that 2021 is going to be an amazing year and that everyone will see much more success! Keep pushing forward, keep fighting, and do not let yourself give up. There is light at the end of the tunnel, and if you are very lucky, perhaps a rainbow as well.

ABOUT THE AUTHOR

Suzanne O'Brien is the CEO of Blake Rian Staffing, which she established in 2018 after spending over 14 years in the staffing industry. With a 15-month-old son at home and one on the way, Suzanne conquered her fear and took a leap of faith by following her dreams of entrepreneurship. She decided to name the company after her soon to be daughter, Blake Rian.

Suzanne took her vision of building meaningful, long-lasting relationships and created a vision for her company. Blake Rian partners with their clients and candidates to truly understand what each side is looking to achieve during the hiring process. She is a firm believer that a resume is important, but it is just a blueprint of someone's experience. She recognizes that by sharing her candidate's story to her clients, they get a better understanding of the value they bring to the table. She brings clarity to her clients, so they gain an understanding of what they really need in an employee, which is not always what the client originally envisioned.

Before founding Blake Rian, Suzanne successfully led teams for some of the largest staffing agencies in Washington and Oregon, including the second-largest global staffing agency. She has found the dream job for tens of thousands of candidates and in turn, helped her clients find the right fit for their teams. Suzanne is very passionate about the Staffing Industry and enjoys building long-lasting relationships with clients and candidates.

Through her journey, she joined the WBENC - Women's Business Enterprise National Council. Suzanne has a passion for empowering women and helping lift them to achieve their goals.

LinkedIn: *www.linkedin.com/in/suzanneobrien*

22

TINA GRAVEL

FROM 5-STAR HOTELS TO 5-HOURS ON ZOOM

"**G**et up, get up, you were supposed to be up at seven! You have overslept all week! What is going on?" I opened my eyes to real concern on my partner's face. "You are not yourself at all. Are you down? Are you depressed?"

It was 8:00 a.m. in Chicago, which means it was 9:00 in the East and work was already percolating for sure. My feelings of lethargy quickly turned to panic as I felt that familiar fear and dread kick in. "Perhaps you should talk to someone about this?" There it was: "Perhaps you should talk to someone about this?" That meant talk to a therapist. There was no fuzz on this; I could no longer hide my "down cycle." If Allen could see it, was evident to everyone?

Three weeks prior, I was at the annual RSA convention in San Francisco staying in a five-star hotel, with meetings from 8:00 in the morning to after dinner time. I guess you could say I was "living large," eating at the best restaurants, staying in beautiful hotels, and often upgraded to fly in first class. I was moving fast, as fast as humanly possible. This was going on most of my career. I also had the blessing of a happy home life, a wonderful fiancé, a soon to be stepdaughter I adore, my dogs. By all outward appearances, you could say I looked like I had it all.

My descent into the dark began in December when my job was eliminated. Though I had recommended a restructuring, I was completely surprised when I learned I would be exiting the business along with the changes I suggested. An executive in a sister company called immediately and offered me a job. I happily accepted it and had no time of unemployment, but as grateful as I was, the situation was unsettling. I wasn't a person that was eliminated in the past. Adding to my concerns was a family member just diagnosed with an illness that could be fatal. I was reeling, but as with many times in the past, I put a big smile on my face and moved on.

My trip to San Francisco that week in February came at the perfect time, it felt so good to be able to be busy and it was as if nothing had really changed. There were reporters and influencers to see; people that wanted my opinion. My friends and former co-workers were there, and it felt like a work reunion of sorts. If anyone asked about what had happened in December, I brushed it off with, "It's all good." Then I ran. Not literally of course, but you can bet I had an excuse that conveniently led me out of that conversation. There were thousands of excuses that day, so much to do and people to see, it was easy to keep moving and not have to share what was really happening or feel any of my own discomfort or pain.

There was rumor of a "virus," we were urged not to shake hands or hug, but we rarely observed these rules. Later, we were told that two gentlemen were affected at the event and one with pre-existing conditions had passed away.

I returned home and within days was told that the next big event I was due to attend in early March was cancelled, then another, and another. I was crestfallen. There were many public speaking opportunities I had looked forward to, including a keynote that I had been planning for months. With each week that went by, another event would cancel. It seemed so unreal. I kept thinking, this would all be over soon, and things would return to normal. I reassured a friend who had lost a job in the travel business. "The experts are saying give it six weeks, it will blow over," I told her. I had read that in a post, probably an opinion or fake news. I so wanted to reassure and make things better for her… and for me.

I hated not traveling. My entire career I traveled for business. I would complain about schedules and traveling; how living that way would play havoc with my routines, etc. but my truth was that I needed to be in motion, ALWAYS. I did not realize I was addicted to the chaos of all the movement and that every relationship in my life reflected that. Over the years, wise individuals recommended meditation and yoga, and I would think to myself, "You really do not know me, do you?" My late parents would remark how I could not, or would not, relax, and it truly worried them. They said I had two speeds: 90 MPH and sleep. I would laugh about this, not knowing how damaging and harmful this was and not understanding that they wanted me to slow down and be present with them. My role models always seemed to work hard and since I was a person of extremely low confidence, I always believed if I ran just a bit farther and faster, I could do as well or maybe even better than you.

I remember one lunch with a supervisor, I apologized to him for finishing first, "I eat too fast!" He said, "Tina you, do everything fast." He knew me well; it was my modus operandi. "To simply out work you, even if it killed me."

That day in March was the first time since the loss of my mother that I really felt that I needed some outside help. But what I did not realize was that a quick reboot would not do the trick. I could not take quick action and get back to normal. A couple of counseling sessions and some retail therapy would not do it for me. The pandemic and subsequent quarantine sent me into an existential crisis. This was the beginning of months of living in stillness and inquiry about my life which I had never, ever done.

I decided to seek medical help, not mental help. Yes, I knew I need a counselor and I told myself I would get to that but if I could get a quick fix that would surely be preferable. Surely there was an anti-depressant, bio-identical hormone or something that could be prescribed for what ailed me? My doctor's response completely floored me, and frankly, angered me too. She replied that she could prescribe medication but would rather not. She would rather I find a "talking" therapist first, then come back to her and if it made sense, they could prescribe something as a team. I called a therapist.

Over the next several months I would learn that,"Yes, I was depressed." I was sleeping too much and eating too much. I was so isolated from my friends and family; all I was really doing was working then retreating to my cocoon of food, mind-numbing internet, television and some family time. My counselor said I was "mourning the death of the life I had," and that made perfect sense to me. I was also quite angry with the situation and my anger had turned inward on myself. Why wasn't I more resilient? Why wasn't I working out like all the people I saw on Instagram? Why didn't I eat better? I realized my self-talk was something that had to change first. I had to stop being angry at myself and eliminate the negative comments toward myself. I needed to become my own best cheerleader. Somehow, I thought if I was the toughest tough love coach around, I could beat myself into anything. I would be my own personal boot camp leader. What I found was that it quickly went from, "You can do it, you got this," to "Why can't you do it?" That had to change.

As the fog of negativity and despair began to lift, I decided I needed to discuss my eating with an expert. I hired a nutritionist who immediately suggested intermittent fasting. I would only eat from noon until seven and thus, I could not graze through the kitchen until bedtime. As the night-time eating stopped, my sleep immediately improved, and it became easier to get up early in the morning. I have since learned that I was "chaining" positive habits together so that they could reinforce each other. The early morning time I found I now enjoyed, allowed me to add in things like prayer and meditation and journaling (or simply writing a gratitude list if I did not feel like journaling). I also added daily workouts. I began to greet my workday, not only more energized, but with a peace about me that helped me be more present for others.

A wise business coach once told me that without first helping yourself, you cannot help others. (At least I remember it that way.) My desire for managing others or leading is to have employees that work for me leave better than when they arrived. The work I was doing on me significantly increased the capacity to serve those that reported to me, my peers, and other co-workers. I was completely transparent with my team about what I was doing to care for myself around the daily practices of sleeping, eating well, moving and meditating. I was not comfortable sharing my experience with therapy, but I did say that my motto was "extreme selfcare" around the quadrants of physical, mental, emotional, and spiritual health. I knew I had changed when sitting quietly was no longer was a curse to me, but now started to feel like a blessing.

If I were to provide advice to anyone embarking on any transformative work, it would be to follow the direction of others. I could not attack this in my typical "Type A" way. If I poured myself into therapy, nutrition improvements, working out regularly, sleeping better and meditation all at once, I surely would have abandoned all of it with the same rigor. I took on small changes one at a time. One week I added drinking more water, another week I simply added more time to the meditation practice. I performed small things that I could track and feel good about. Once those were mastered, I added more small practices and little improvements. The pandemic and quarantine felt like walking in quicksand, everything I did felt harder than it normally would. I felt that I was barely able to do what I had to do, let alone all the things that I wanted to do. Starting slowly was not really a choice, when I am honest with myself about it.

My team is greeted by a human being that has mostly great days now. Though I still have bad days like anyone, I try not to share that with them. I know that many of them still struggle with the weight of COVID-19, and any and every other stress that could be applied on them. Perhaps they lack one of the two incomes they depended on, sick relatives that cannot be seen, home schooling, etc. I am grateful I can really be present and ask them how they are doing and if I see a glimmer of something not quite right, I can offer an ear or some other assistance. This is not something I would have done previously. I would be far too busy being busy and would have waited until they came to me, unable to pick up on their cues as I was moving far too fast. Now that I know there is likely to be an outside stressor, their one-on-one sessions with me are often about blowing off steam and laughing together first, then work matters second. We also have laughter and a bit of silliness from time to time in our group meetings. The tension we are all living with is so high, if I can help throttle it back at work a bit, I know that they will be happier and perform better.

I remember one of the best examples of this. I asked one of my brightest, highest-performing team members a simple question one-on-one, "How are you really doing? I am not wondering about your work, but what about everything else?" That question led to an emotional discussion about the tension at home, issues of home schooling, COVID-19 diagnoses all around the family, financial stressors. I said, "Look, your work product is great. If you need to put the work down early, stop working. Do what you need to do to care for you. You won't have anything left for your family or your job unless you take a breather." I wanted to lessen the pressure as I knew the person had very little reserves left in the "bank of life."

Another noticeable difference in our work today is evident when a dog or child shows up during a Zoom call. Now, as a rule, we invite them in for a quick "Hello," not rushing them away. It adds something lovely most of the time. Once, during a tough session with an employee when her dog showed up in the frame I said, "Oh, why not go ahead and hug your dog, it looks like you might need a hug," and she did, and it helped.

The energy, coping skills, and stamina were not just shared with my staff but with everyone I encountered in the company. I tried to remain upbeat but sincere in my concern. I made close friendships with other women at my level in the company and we started to speak regularly about our personal challenges. Recognizing the benefit of this, a dear friend and fellow senior leader and I created the Women of Appgate so that all the other women in the company could join us on a weekly basis to discuss issues, have a bit of fun (we sometimes played remote games), or just share concerns. We were urged by HR to NOT make it about business, to really try to get beyond the job in this group and it worked really well. When racial issues were exploding all over the country, it was within this group that I was able to show concern, ask and truly understand how it must have felt for a Black American to see George Floyd die on camera.

I received management training at a large outsourcing company in the 1980s. The company was full of former military and our badge colors reflected it. I was the lowest rank, so I had a green badge; the seas parted when a gold badged executive entered the room. I have to chuckle when I think back at the rules. One item: women had to wear hose that were nude color only. These were the days of wearing a suit that was as close to a replica of a man's, even down to the bowtie at the neck (except we had a skirt to go with the hideous hose!) My way of leading was always about control and chain of command, after all, that was how I was taught. The leadership that the pandemic required was all about transparency and flexibility. I was a bit uncomfortable with it at first, but it was absolutely required and luckily, I adapted fast.

My relationship with my family is deeper than ever. The time in quarantine with my "soon to be" stepdaughter was a blessing I never dreamed I could have. Instead of simply getting moments of time as I dropped her at one event or another, we spent lots of time together cooking and doing activities. As I came out of my fog, I was able to be present for her and her frustrations as well. My partner is very grateful for the work I have done, he thinks it has benefited him well and tells me how proud he is of me all the time.

I am grateful that the lack of travel became a catalyst for me to look at myself and my life. I am most grateful that this work has allowed me to be of service to others. When you aren't at your best, it is difficult to have the energy you need for yourself, let alone your family or friends. However, I would not have wished for this pandemic to happen in order to allow for my transformation. A dear friend of mine lost her husband in April, before they knew how to properly treat this monster disease. She was also hospitalized for two months due to COVID-19. My gratitude knows no bounds, and I am working hard to support others that have financial and other needs and I urge others to do the same. Though we may all be experiencing this pandemic, we are not experiencing things in the same way. I completely acknowledge this, and I am working hard to do whatever I can to help others that still suffer daily.

My goals, as written in March of 2020, were to be "emotionally sound, mentally strong, physically fit, and spiritually healthy." None of that was familiar to me at the moment I wrote that, but as I write this in November 2020, I can tell you that as early as this summer, my life was fun and bright again by every single measure on those quadrants.

You might be wondering if my work performance suffered while I focused on my transformation. My team and I have excelled despite the issues that have made our lives more difficult. I eliminated time spent on online shopping, social media, and television. The time spent on healthy habits just means I spend less time on activities I really do not need. If you had told me to stop traveling for two months to focus on myself, I never would have done it, let alone eight months. But even two months would have been a wonderful restart for me. This time has taught me that my leadership skills are only as good as my personal health and wellness.

To be the best leader, I had to lead myself first.

ABOUT THE AUTHOR

For 27 years, Tina Gravel has been a "road warrior" serving in various capacities for many technology companies. However, nothing had prepared her for what would happen when her wings were clipped on March 8, 2020. She was forced to sit still and learn how to lead in the stillness and sameness of quarantine time. Her chapter, "From 5-Star Hotels to 5 Hours on Zoom," tells the story of how Tina had to change and adapt to a new way of leading, not just for her team, but also, for herself.

An award-winning executive with more than 27 years of experience in information technology, Tina is currently Senior Vice President of Global Channels and Alliances with Appgate, a cybersecurity software and services company. Tina is widely known as a cybersecurity influencer and has received countless awards for her work in the technology channel including the Top Gun 51 Channel Chief award by Channel Online in 2019. In 2020, Tina was named #58 on a Global list of IIOT influencers by Onalytica and as a Top 50 Women in Tech Globally by Award Magazine.

Tina resides in Chicago, with her fiancé and his teenage daughter, along with the family's two dogs. Her passion is working with other women on issues of equality and fairness, diversity, and inclusion. She serves on the advisory boards of Cloud Girls and the Alliance of Channel Women and is a proud co-founder of the Women of Appgate.

Website: www.tinagravel.com
LinkedIn: www.linkedin.com/in/tinagravel
Twitter: www.twitter.com/tgravel
Email: tgravel536@gmail.com

23

VIVIAN CINTRON

RESILIENCE... THE ABILITY TO ADAPT AND BOUNCE FORWARD

When I was called in to be part of the task force of COVID-19 at the American Red Cross Indiana Region on March 5th, I was surrounded by a group of peers and leaders—among them physicians, emergency responders, and healthcare professionals.

At the beginning of the meeting, the President of the American Red Cross Indiana Region asked me to provide information about the COVID-19 virus since he knew the science of infectious diseases was my expertise. As I started explaining the mechanism of its virulence and how it would spread, I saw the fear in the eyes of the members sitting around the table, and they fell into deep silence, listening to the news of this inevitable pandemic.

I was relaying the scientific facts and almost forgetting my audience. I panicked for a moment thinking I overdid my summary and that I should have just started with a brief description of the virus and in simple terms, what to expect without emphasizing the gravity of it. As I looked around the table, I remembered this was not any other table of peers and leaders, this was the American Red Cross; the most resilient of the organizations that have always been there to lead the path to help the community and show support in hard times. Towards the end of my discussion, I shared with the team, "We got this...this is the American Red Cross." This Organization has helped during previous pandemics because we have found ways to help people when impossible is not part of the options. Tornados, hurricanes, wildfires, and snow storms have not prevented the American Red Cross from offering support in a disaster. We have always been there to adapt, reinvent ways, and lend a hand to our community in need. With that new mind, the leaders around the table reviewed the protocols to be implemented during the pandemic, utilizing the updates from the World Health Organization (WHO) and the Center for Disease Control and Prevention's (CDC) guidance. The Task Force reviewed one of the American Red Cross' main priorities: support our communities while also ensuring the safety of our staff members and volunteers. During these unprecedented times, the American Red Cross prepared to serve as a catalyst for social service in the community by partnering with the healthcare and other agencies to build resilience. The group turned to identify blind spots by asking questions and thinking about how to communicate clearly.

At this time in early March of 2020, the American Red Cross Indiana Region learned that we were under the American Red Cross Operational response, after recognizing guidance from the CDC that there was a confirmation of multiple human cases, indicating efficient and sustained human-to-human transmission with potential for a pandemic and determination for a potential Public Health Emergency. The full range of disaster cycle services were going to continue to be provided by the American Red Cross; however, without requiring direct contact with patients confirmed with COVID-19. In addition, the American Red Cross needed to start implementing disaster workforce infection control procedures as part of the administrative rules, hygiene, work practices and appropriate protective equipment utilization when needed as support at congregate sites of masses.

During this meeting, we learned quickly that the Emergency Medical Services were going to utilize screening questions during the initial help calls. As a team, we discussed the consideration of utilizing the same triage questions at the American Red Cross Indiana Region responders and dispatch lines by asking, "Do you have flu like symptoms, or does someone in your household have flu like symptoms? Have you been sick in the last few days?" before going into the homes. For instance, when a person needed a shelter, we partnered with the Indiana Department of

Health as part of the deployment policy, not exposing our staff to COVID-19-infected community members, and helping the community when shelter was needed. It was part of the Disaster Cycle Service and Task Force at the American Red Cross to look at how this was going to be implemented. First, we would receive an appointment request. Then the Health Department was going to perform a test screening before admitting the person to a shelter facility. The team started considering other programs that needed periodic home visits. For example, "sound the alarm programs" are where the American Red Cross visits homes to exchange batteries on smoke detectors, saving many lives annually. We were going to innovate and "call into homes" by utilizing volunteers to phone the community residents and to check if anything was needed, to look out for one another during this pandemic in our community!

After the meeting ended, I drove back home. I felt incredible emotion. A feeling of the unknown. A fear of the future and uncertainty I have only felt once before in my lifetime...during the events of September 11, 2001. As I was driving home through the streets of Indianapolis, I started to see the faces of people in the cars next to me; faces of desolation and despair. The streets were almost vacant, like a winter storm alert where only essential traffic is allowed on the streets, and this was only the beginning of the pandemic. How long was this storm going to last?

Once I reached home and through the following days, my mind raced at a hundred miles per hour. How can a disaster agency like the American Red Cross work virtually? How could the American Red Cross Indiana Region reinvent the community outreach programs to continue offering support? Immediately, many meetings were organized, and ideas started flowing and programs started reaching our communities.

As the pandemic escalated in March and April, the American Red Cross Indiana Region saw that people's mental health was declining, and we needed to do something. I often found myself listening to the everyday calls of peers telling me about the healthcare tolls, the family reaction to the isolation, and the empty spirits of the unknown during the pandemic. The American Red Cross Indiana Region partnered with the Indiana State Department of Health to offer a series of free online psychological courses, which provided practical instructions on how to support others during stressful situations. This gave the opportunity to hundreds of Hoosiers to enroll in these courses. I registered many friends, peers and family for these classes, which helped them realize that things would get better. The American Red Cross Indiana Region adapted and offered Resilience workshops for military members and families through a virtual delivery platform as well. These workshops were led by Indiana-based licensed mental health therapists to help service members, veterans, and families manage the stress of isolation, navigate challenges associated with working and schooling from home, and promote healthy sleep and relaxation practices.

By mid-March, the process of clinical isolation started. The virus was not widespread in all hospitals, and infection prevention protocols were in place, some of them following previous H1N1 and SARS pandemics, but COVID-19 was more transmissible. Some of the protocols were COVID-19 testing performed by the Public Health Department, contact tracing, distancing, hand washing, and face coverings to prevent the spread of the virus.

Alarmingly, COVID-19 created several challenges for our nation's blood supply. During the American Red Cross Indiana Region BioMed Committee, of which I am also a member, the news of the need for blood donations was distressing. It was already the end of March and all major events for donations at schools, churches and corporations were cancelled due to the pandemic. The schools started to close, and classes changed to virtual events. Most of the corporate work was transferred to home base. How could we find donors or alert donors to come to one location to donate during a pandemic? This was a situation never experienced before, and there was always a need for blood for critical patients or emergencies.

The American Red Cross campaign to donate blood started to circulate throughout the US, stressing the safety of the donation process during the pandemic, following the CDC guidance, where face coverings were utilized at all times and measures to prevent virus infection were part of the protocols, including the use of protective equipment by healthcare workers and distance requirements. The American Red Cross immediately provided an easy online registration to enter contact information followed by simple questions. An American Red Cross health staff was able to call those community members that wanted to donate blood and asked specific questions for eligibility, and other questions related to COVID-19 exposures, for example any contact with a COVID-19 infected person, or travels to a high-risk area or experienced illness or symptoms related to COVID-19. After all the information was entered, a donation appointment was confirmed with the donor as well as sharing a map for the location of the donation facilities.

But where was the American Red Cross Indiana Region going to find a big space to have these donations since school gyms and corporate offices were closed? In addition, how were we going to alert the community that this space was open on a specific day of the week? I felt a rush of blood in my head (no pun intended) as I was thinking of a solution. I needed to help by providing ideas for blood drives, or how to attract community participation. I thought about bringing the American Red Cross Donation Unit—which is a big mobile unit equipped with instruments for blood collections ready to be driven anywhere at any time. However, the mobile unit had limitations in terms of capacity for individuals donating, and some individuals needed to wait outside until the current donor completed the donation, exposing them to the cold of winter. This was not a viable solution. Another idea was to utilize another location close to several communities where members could donate. But how could we afford to rent the location for blood donation?

I started communications with the American Red Cross Indiana Region Account Manager and exchanged discussions on these ideas. Immediately, she looked into locations and I concentrated efforts on finding the people who were willing to donate. I created a simple post for my neighborhood in the Nextdoor Social Media application, explaining the need for blood donations due to the limited supply of blood during the pandemic. I expected ten people to answer my post since I thought people were in fear of leaving their homes due to the coronavirus. I received the first community response five minutes after the post, asking to be added to a list. I contacted the person immediately and explained that as soon as I had confirmation of the address, I would provide the information for the drive location in addition to the registration link for the donation appointment. Two other neighbors contacted me within the next five minutes, and I explained the same information.

Incredibly, I had never met all the neighbors in my community, and I thought this would be a great exercise. For the next thirty minutes, I answered more than fifty people that contacted me regarding information on how to donate. In an hour, I had 100 members of my community committed to donate. I could not believe it! Most of the residents told me that they felt hopeless and isolated and were looking for a way to help someone in need, and this call to donate blood was what lifted them to support other people. The following day, I opened the Nextdoor invitation to the other neighboring communities, and in two days, 300 people signed for a two-day donation event. During this time, the Account Manager received a positive call from a store at a nearby outdoor shopping mall that closed down. We could utilize it for the donation at no cost. Immediately, the American Red Cross Indiana Region staff members got to work, identifying healthcare workers, screeners, technicians, and administrative staff for this location. Within a week, this location was transformed into a blood donation center, with equipment, isolation areas, one route traffic, distancing stations, face covering requirements and all protective gear to welcome donations during the COVID-19 pandemic. This was a monster of a project made in a week!

The two days of blood collections were flawless. Healthcare workers worked on a rotational basis to prevent exhaustion. Members of the community were screened for their temperatures and welcomed to the facilities following strict protocols on face coverings, distance requirements, and hygiene. I was there to see the public show their happiness through the corners of their eyes—the only part of the face that you could see because they were all wearing their face coverings, which have become the fashion trend for the year 2020—you could tell they were smiling. Most of them expressed how grateful they were to have this opportunity do something good for those in need of blood during the COVID-19 pandemic. Each of the donors and healthcare workers received a gift card for a pizza from a local restaurant, as gratitude from the American Red Cross. It was an incredible feeling to know the resilience in our community amid COVID-19. People wanted to help each other!

As new COVID-19 infection continued along the months, the American Red Cross continued to reinvent programs for the community. During a Disaster Cycle Services, the American Red Cross handled blankets, water, snacks, and other supplies, and this time it was no different, except with the appropriate CDC guidance. What else could the American Red Cross provide? An amazing group of volunteers at the American Red

Cross Indiana Region started sewing face coverings for the community residents in need and gradually, this program produced 40,750 face coverings by the end of September, 2020. Incredibly, this program originated in 1918 during the Influenza pandemic, and was now revived in the times of COVID-19.

The American Red Cross achieved resilience by adapting other programs during the pandemic. The Indiana Region was among the first regions in the United States to join a Virtual Family Assistance Center pilot program that provided access to a range of integrated care and condolence services to those dealing with the death of a loved one from COVID-19. The American Red Cross licensed mental health and other health professionals developed the site in close collaboration with dozens of social, faith-based, and veterans services throughout Indiana. These resources were developed also in a paper-based version and distributed in churches, funeral homes and directly to impacted families.

The work of the American Red Cross continues as the pandemic evolves. As a volunteer and board member, I am dedicated to amplify the message to control COVID-19 infections, to educate the community about the influenza season and its vaccination, as well as preparedness in education as soon as COVID-19 vaccination information is available. Incredible people have worked above and beyond to develop programs in The American Red Cross, educating the community on "Returning to Work During COVID-19: Safe Work Practices," an online course based on guidance from the CDC and the US Occupational Safety and Health Administration (OSHA).

I have lived through natural disasters such as hurricanes, floods, earthquakes, and tornados, and I have seen how the American Red Cross has helped my community by providing basic human needs. Growing up, I remember a story my mom used to tell me. She narrated that in 1960, during a tempest, a young police officer was called to help evacuate people from the path of the main river in my hometown. The night of the storm, an elderly woman sent her daughter—a young lady—to the shelter with food for the American Red Cross volunteers, who were helping the evacuees all day, nonstop. As this young lady walked into the shelter, she saw the chaos and desperation of people to be relocated quickly out of the path of the swelling river and helped with the American Red Cross team, moving evacuees from the police cars, and from the American Red Cross trucks into the shelter. During one of these trips, she met the young police officer and together that night, they helped many people relocate safely to the shelter. This is the story of how my mom met my dad. The American Red Cross has always been a powerful image in my community and influence in my life with the message of, "We are here to help." My current role as a Board Member of the American Red Cross Indiana Region, Task Force member and volunteer is to bring this organization to the community and to help identify the needs where the American Red Cross could assist. I am grateful to be part of this organization that brings so much comfort to the community.

The COVID-19 pandemic has shown how we have been able to adapt to adversities and bounce back from the unknown of a new virus to provide innovations, solutions and reinvent a way of life for the existence of humanity." Being part of the American Red Cross has shown me how to be resilient, to be adaptable, and to move forward because nothing prepares you for the unknown of a new virus, where all these innovations come out of necessity.

ABOUT THE AUTHOR

Dr. Cintron is a molecular biologist and geneticist with over twenty-five years of global experience in medical and scientific affairs. She holds an Executive Leadership Certification from Cornell University, is a former US Army Reserve Captain, completed postdoctoral trainings at NIH and Eli Lilly, and obtained her MBA.

Before the age of fifteen, Dr. Cintron won several national and international Scientific Fair Awards. Science is her passion and she loves to experiment.

She is the founder of Viony Consultants LLC, where she provides consultations to pharmaceuticals, biotechnologies and healthcare organizations. She also serves as a board member of the Red Cross at Indianapolis, and as a member of the Red Cross COVID-19 Task Force. In her chapter, Dr. Cintron shares how *resilience* is the specific trait of humankind that will help us move forward in this pandemic. Nothing in life prepares you for the unknown of a new virus, and she believes that the best innovations come out of necessity

Dr. Cintron lives in Indiana and enjoys spending quality time with her husband, Tony, and dog, Kronos. Her extraordinary experience and career are only topped by her driven and upbeat personality and her contagious positive attitude.

LinkedIn: *www.linkedin.com/in/dr-vivian-cintron-24140b8/*

24

WYATT KNIGHT

1% BETTER EVERYDAY

The hamster wheel has stopped, the reality of your life kicks in, you have a moment to pause and reflect, you have a chance to look in the mirror to see who you are.

What do you see? Do you see someone that is inspiring yourself to get a little better every day? Do you see someone who is a leader in their own life? Do you see someone who is walking their talk? For many of us, these are questions we have had to face in this pivotal moment in human history. The year 2020 has been a time of immense reflection, deep judgement of oneself, and a newfound vigor to enact long-lasting changes throughout our dated societal institutions.

The world has changed, society has changed, and the concept of leadership has changed. The real question then becomes, have you changed? Have you said to yourself: *I am ready to lead my own life, to not look to others to solve my problems. I know that the better world I desire starts with making hard decisions about who I am and what I stand for in my life?* Those societal institutions that have been questioned, challenged, and altered forever this year were built to make decisions for the masses, a concept that we can no longer stand for, a belief that we must change by continuing our internal search within.

As the founder of The 1% Better Club, a virtual human empowerment program launched at the height of the pandemic, these are a few of the founding ideas that we are consistently looking at to understand and take action on by aligning our mind, body, and soul through mindset, nutrition, and fitness. Through this alignment, our club members focus on becoming the leaders of their own lives before focusing on leading others in their work, communities, and at home.

As the world went into limbo, as our leaders stumbled, as our communities shattered, many questioned if we could move forward from such a challenging human experience. Through great challenges come great opportunities for leaders to emerge, for real change to be enacted, for a brighter future to form under these unique circumstances. The power of 2020 comes from the fascinating concept that the entire human race has 'struggled' during this year and felt the effects of the pandemic in every corner of the world. This universal struggle brings about the ability to have universal change, when everyone wants change, everyone has a chance to become a leader, and leading yourself is the first step in the right direction.

This macro and micro way of looking at the potential to enact lasting change comes from my personal experiences working in Harlem, New York and Eastern Kentucky—two historically opportunity-deprived communities in our country that demand true *internal* leadership. As my team and I built out empowerment programs in these communities, the same question continually needed an answer, "How do we make real change in areas that have been unable to see real change for generations?" Through years of tireless work, consistent error and glimmers of hope, we found the answer always was, and always will be, "You empower one person at a time to be the leader of their own lives." If you want to *end* poverty in Eastern Kentucky or empower the inner city youth of Harlem, you unconditionally support one person at a time in their process of mind, body, soul alignment to be the change they wish to see in themselves. That one individual's ability to enact real change in their lives has a ripple effect in their friend group, in their family, in their schools, and throughout their communities. By leading themselves, others will follow. As others follow, a better world emerges.

I first met Souleymane Ballo in 2012 as a young, friendly, skinny seventh-grader in a failing middle school in a struggling part of Harlem, New York. As I helped establish Harlem Lacrosse, an at-risk youth empowerment program, I struggled to launch the program meant to support those in need of consistent empowerment in their lives and desperately needed a leader to emerge within the group of young men aimlessly roaming the halls. At the time, 'Souley', as he is affectionately called, was living in a two bedroom apartment with his parents and seven older sisters as his immigrant parents worked tirelessly to stay above the poverty line. As I patrolled the hallways, begging students to join the program, down the hall emerged Souley with a look of determination I will never forget.

That look, and his words, were a turning point in my life, a turning point in his life, his family's life, his friend's life, his school's path, and his community's potential forever. "Coach, I wanted to let you know that I decided to fully commit to your program. I know it is the best way to get me and my family out of poverty and I will do whatever it takes to succeed and help you build out this program at school." At that moment, Souley became the leader of his own life and took on the unique challenge of being the leader for forty other young at-risk youth in need of real leadership to alter the trajectory of their lives and the community as a whole. When leaders emerge, by committing to leading themselves, others will follow. When others follow, a stronger community emerges.

Fast forward eight years later and Souleymane has consistently taken the next step in his leadership evolution to be the change he wishes to see in himself, through his friend groups, in his community and with his family. Currently on a full scholarship—playing Division 1 Lacrosse at Hobart College—Souley is working numerous jobs to keep himself financially stable. He is running the alumni outreach program for Harlem Lacrosse to stay connected with his teammates and is seeking prestigious internships in the summer months to focus on building out businesses that continue to redefine what it means to be a young man born in Harlem. Being the leader of your own life means you are blazing a trail that has never been taken, you are experiencing experiences that have never been experienced, you are arriving at questions that may not have answers to. I would like to strongly suggest, even encourage you, to blaze your trail. To experience things that have never been experienced. To work tirelessly to answer the questions that need answers. You may ask, "Why?" and the answer is clear; what has not yet been discovered, experienced and answered *inside* of you, is exactly what the world needs to become a better version of itself.

My experience with Souleymane is at the very foundation of my belief that real, lasting, genuine change starts and ends with one person at a time emerging as the leader of his or her own life's journey. If you want to change your life, commit to yourself. If you want to change your community, lead others by leading yourself. If you want to make the world a better place, make yourself a better person. Souleymane is one person—who made one decision—that is now at the forefront of bringing an entire community out of poverty and in a position to propel our country forward into the next phase of inclusive growth and organic prosperity.

As I launched The 1% Better Club in the early months of the global pandemic, I often thought of the saying, "be the change you wish to see in the world." As humans, we often "hope" for change. As humans, we often struggle with change. As humans, we often find it easier to change others, than to change ourselves. Throughout this trying year, it has become obvious that hoping for change, struggling with change and pointing fingers at others to change is exactly how we put ourselves in the position we are in today. Internal reflection and change is a difficult and worthy journey to go on, just as it should be.

In The 1% Better Club, we build mental, physical, and nutritional habits centered on combating the struggles of change to help each individual maximize their potential to be the leaders of their own lives. Change is difficult, no matter how you handle it. However, having a plan with your change process, being in control of your mind, moving your body, and connecting with your soul daily, will allow you to understand your change, guide your change, and maximize it to maximize you.

Many of our members join the club to take back ownership of their lives. When we live in a society focused on altering the masses, we often feel neglected, distrustful, and frustrated at not seeing the results we want in our lives, hence the problem with allowing others to dictate your life's path. For most of our lives, we are told to attend certain schools, to work certain jobs, to focus on certain careers, to eat certain foods. That standard that society has built for us—mostly fueled by financial gains—does not allow us the opportunity to take a moment, breathe and ask ourselves, "Is *this* my path"? The magic of 2020, and the real leadership change that is emerging in one person at a time, is based on that universal pause we have experienced. We now have a moment to reflect, and realize that the schools, jobs, careers, foods, friends and life we have been given might need some drastic changes to live the life we want. We now have a moment to say, "Ahhh, *this* is my path."

Finding your path and living your path are two separate processes that require continually altering your current habits and routines. Finding your path is the inward search we have discussed in brief above, that process of looking into the mirror and asking the hard questions while taking action on the steps to self improvement. Mostly, this process needs to take place by yourself, with the focus being listening to the little voice in your head saying, "this way." This will be the hardest part of your journey, the search within, because there are no right or wrong answers. There is no one perfect path and no guidelines for finding your path. Living your path is where The 1% Better Club comes into full empowerment mode and gives you the extra push needed to maximize your potential in life.

Living your path, which for many in The 1% Better Club, is being the leader of their own lives, requires first breaking down two concepts; your time and energy. These two concepts are at the very center of everything we do in our lives. Time is the finite period we have as human beings on planet earth. Energy is what we do during that finite period on planet earth. The more we focus on being in control of our time and energy, the more we begin to take back control of our time and energy and place it in areas that make you a better version of yourself. The path to accomplishing what you want in your life is inserting focused energy into uninterrupted time. Leaders obsess over these two concepts to put themselves consistently in the best position to maximize their impact on the world, on others, and themselves. Continually focus on putting your time and energy into people, ideas, and experiences that make you a better version of yourself and you will continually put yourself in the best position to live your best life.

As the club members take back control of their time and energy, we focus on reinserting it into areas that will maximize their potential in life; their mind, body, and soul. The thoughts you put into your mind, the food you put into your body, the way you move your body, and your life's purpose that guides your soul are the pillars of your leadership journey.

The time and energy that you insert into your mind, body and soul is a direct correlation to the person you are and the person you are focused on becoming.

I am continually fascinated by the power of consistent self-improvement and the ability it has to be the change we wish to see in the world. The mind, body and soul alignment is a crucial step in one's leadership journey that has a ripple effect throughout the entire world. If you are focused on getting 1% Better every day, an immediate action item would be to go find the closest mirror. Once at the mirror, look back at yourself, and ask, "Who am I? What do I want to accomplish in my life? What is holding me back?" (Maintain eye contact the entire time). Whether you have the answers ready or need more time to think them through, you are always welcomed to join The 1% Better Club to maximize your time and energy as a human being on planet earth. Now, go be the change you wish to see in the world.

ABOUT THE AUTHOR

Wyatt Knight is the founder and CEO of W. Knight Ventures, a platform focused on expanding human potential. Wyatt believes in a world where every human strives to be 1% better every day.

Wyatt has spent nearly a decade founding, supporting, and participating in groundbreaking programs focused on empowering humans to maximize their potential in life. He holds a B.A. from The University of Virginia and is a 2011 Division 1 Lacrosse National Champion.

Wyatt has been engaged with transformational organizations breaking down societal barriers in communities such as Harlem, NY; Hazard, KY; and NoMa, DC. After growing up in Ft. Lauderdale, FL, Wyatt has lived and learned in VA, NY, KY, DC and now resides and empowers others in Austin, TX with his wife and two Border Collies.

You are invited to maximize your potential in life by participating in his signature program, The 1% Better Club.

Website: www.wknight-ventures.com
LinkedIn: www.linkedin.com/in/wyattcknight
Instagram: www.instagram.com/wyattcknight
Email: wck@wknightventures.com

ABOUT THE PUBLISHER

Kayleigh Marie O'Keefe is the CEO and Founder of Soul Excellence Publishing where she helps corporate leaders and entrepreneurs express their authentic selves through multi-author books, solo books, and one-on-one personal consulting.

She works with leaders who want to expand their impact and influence, attract new opportunities with ease, and create a more fulfilling life on a day-to-day basis using her signature Soul Excellence Leadership framework. Kayleigh also hosts 'The Kayleigh O'Keefe Show' podcast where she shares her ideas related to personal growth and the future of society and interviews leaders from across a variety of different fields.

Prior to founding the company, Kayleigh spent nearly a decade as a researcher and consultant for Fortune 500 communications executives with CEB (now Gartner) and as a sales and customer success leader at Snapdocs, a Series-C real estate technology company backed by Sequoia Capital and Y Combinator Continuity Fund. She received her B.A. from Duke University and her M.B.A. on a full scholarship from the University of San Francisco.

Kayleigh has walked over four hundred miles across two different routes of The Way of St. James pilgrimage through Spain and Portugal.

After spending most of her career in Washington, D.C. and San Francisco, CA, she now lives and creates by the beach in Ft. Lauderdale, FL.

You are invited to apply to contribute to an upcoming leadership book or to work with Kayleigh one-on-one in her signature program, The Soul Excellence Leadership Accelerator.

> *Website:* www.kayleighokeefe.com
> *LinkedIn:* www.linkedin.com/in/kayleighokeefe
> *Podcast:* www.kayleighokeefe.com/the-kayleigh-okeefe-
>   show-podcast
> *Instagram:* www.instagram.com/KayleighOK_11
> *Email:* kayleigh@kayleighokeefe.com

Made in the USA
Monee, IL
17 December 2021

85919549R00144